From Autism to All-Star

RHONDA BRUNETT

Specialty Publishing Company

ISBN 0-9755199-1-3

Library of Congress Cataloging-in-Publication Data
First Edition

Printed in the United States of America
10 9 8 7 6 5 4 3 2 1

From Autism to All-Star
Printed and designed by Specialty Publishing Company.

Specialty Publishing Company, Inc.
135 E. St. Charles Rd., Carol Stream, Il 60188
www.specialtypub.com

Cover art and design by Deb Donnelly debili@aol.com
www.print2paint.com

Specialty Publishing books are available at special quantity discounts to use as premiums or for corporate educational training programs. For more information, please contact Special Books Manager at 630-933-0844.

To Jordan,
if it wasn't for him I wouldn't be sharing
our journal with the world.

TABLE OF CONTENTS

Foreword

Autism is often confusing, even for me as Jordan's mom. As you'll read, it can bring you to the extremes of all emotions … especially frustration. My hope is that sharing the experiences about my son Jordan will allow someone else to walk away with hope.

Perhaps the comments within, or maybe this book itself, will make its way into the hands of those who can in some way benefit. Maybe a teacher or parent will read this book and it will assist them to better relate to, or recognize, the words and frustrations of another teacher or parent. To look back at what our friends, family, and teachers have expressed, many have noted that they can only imagine what it must have been like to be really alone when dealing with this disorder. As I now look back and see that although I was blessed to have the all-important support system, I still felt so very much alone.

You'll soon discover that I've detailed all the nuts and bolts of our journey and it has resulted in an extraordinary educational experience for us all. If Autism to All-Star can answer just one question or serve as a source of optimism, maybe others won't have to feel as isolated in their journey.

Acknowledgments

I want to start by thanking God for blessing Rick and I with the most awesome son. Jordan is forever astounding us with his continuous gifts. I am thankful for his gifts of great compassion for others and his unending sense of humor, both of these from his dad.

Next, I'd like to thank everyone who has placed themselves on Jordan's path in his lifetime. Our friends, family, neighbors, Jordan's teachers, medical professionals, assistants, and coaches have all made a difference that we will forever be indebted to.

We were also blessed with babysitters who "followed the rules" where Jordan was concerned. Because interactive play was vital when spending time with Jordan, these "angels" constantly played with flashcards and read to Jordan. Thank you Kristina, Mandy, Jill, Dana, Swati, Manisha, Niki, and Mili. Without you, our lives and our ship would have sunk!

It was my insightful friend Ebby who first saw the writing of a three-year-old little boy scrawled on our leather kitchen chair and recognized it as a springboard for this book. Although I wasn't planning to write a book, I did mention to Ebby that I kept a journal throughout my pregnancy, and after, which documented every detail of Jordan's progress. When I spoke to her about the video library recording all of his developmental stages, I wondered if I myself had on some level, been preparing to write a book. I thank Ebby for letting me know it was the right thing to do and the right time.

I would be remiss to not also give special thanks to a special teacher. Surprisingly it is not one of Jordan's teachers…but one of mine! Miss Smith, my fifth grade teacher at Glen Hill School in Glendale Heights, Illinois was a major influence in my life. At a time when I was struggling, Miss Smith impressed upon me that whatever I put my mind to—I could achieve. I've kept her words with me and they have served as a positive force throughout my life.

And so it goes, I share the travels that our family is on. We've each experienced our own frustrations, searching, isolation, understanding, and learning. We've managed to come through it all with love and faith as a family unit. I couldn't even imagine where Rick and I would be without this experience called "parenthood" with our exceptional son, Jordan. You all have our sincerest and warmest gratitude. It is my intention and hope that everyone who reads this book comes away with something for someone.

I would also like to thank Elyse Piper, Ebby Salinas, Deb Donnelly, and Peggy Smedley. Without you four women in my life who gave unselfishly of your time, this book wouldn't be possible. I am forever grateful.

I would like to extend a special thanks to Phillip Leischner who did a fabulous job creating the Web pages www.autism2allstar.com, and Wendy Williams, who keeps it updated and running. You are the best. Thank you from the bottom of my heart.

Preface by Ebby Salinas

Since meeting Rhonda and her family a few years ago, I've been continuously impressed from the very beginning with the way in which they moved forward as a family unit. I looked forward to hearing my "Jordan stories" and would often call Rhonda to get the latest updates.

I've never been exposed to anyone with autism, and although I met Rhonda when Jordan was already integrated into groups, the education I received was invaluable. I wasn't aware of DNA drives and politics, Motorcycle Runs, Cure Autism Now—CAN, The Doug Flutie Jr. Foundation, etc. I wasn't aware how many people are actually out there everyday working hard to help discover the "hows and whys" of a disorder which must be cured.

I've learned that on a personal level, the children afflicted must be given every possible chance to overcome this with early diagnosis and screening. But most important,

I've learned that although I did not previously know of anyone personally diagnosed with autism other than Jordan Brunett, it has enabled me to become more aware and involved—to feel like I do know a lot of...Jordan Brunetts. We all need to make this cause and cure "personal." I give my thanks to Rhonda Brunett, for making this personal for me.

Excerpt Friend Elyse Piper

Kids...what do I know? Autism...what do I know? Apparently, not much about either! In fact, it was only after I had the opportunity to preview Rhonda's book that I got a huge dose of reality. What I do know is that I have an enormous respect for Rhonda and how she and Rick endeavored, explored, insisted, and endured.

When I began visiting the Brunett household for my monthly hair appointments in about 2000, what I observed was an adorable young boy with tousled blonde hair, a contagious smile, and non-stop energy. Rhonda at some point had mentioned as an FYI that Jordan was diagnosed as "autistic," but outwardly he appeared to be a normal, over-active kid. On many visits, he had endless energy and was somewhat rambunctious. "Couldn't mom and dad control him?" I ignorantly wondered.

Then there were those times that Jordan would amaze me with his mathematical genius. He would instantly calculate dates, ages, and birth years. I had heard of savants and thought, "Is this how Jordan's autism presents itself? From what I see, he's been blessed with special gifts and talents." Of course, I hadn't a clue about those agonizing years of non-communication, meltdowns, frustration, and desperation that Rhonda and everyone around her had experienced. Not being aware of what went on behind the scenes, I am truly in awe of how Rhonda and Rick always presented themselves with such a calm demeanor.

Jordan's integration into regular classes and leading a "normal" life at the level he enjoys today was not automatic. It didn't merely just happen. It took years of painstaking and constant commitment. As an outsider, what I sometimes perceived as a doting, overly concerned and pushy (at-school-with-teachers) mom was the tireless spirit, will, intuition, and fortitude of a loving mother selflessly acting as Jordan's advocate. She wouldn't have had it any other way.

This book is not only a true, unaltered expression of a mother's inner-most feelings, but an account and timeline of Jordan's struggles, growth, and victory to overcome his Autistic behavior. Rhonda is one of the most devoted and patient mothers I will ever know and it's an honor to be her friend.

1

What's Taking You So Long?

<u>First Journal Entry</u>

Talking to my baby's soul up there in heaven. What's taking you so long Jordan?* Is there a traffic jam? I'm waiting to meet you again. I heard we had many lifetimes together. I'll be here for you and I'm so excited to meet you. I hope you're not away much longer, we have so much to do. Love Mommy.

*I always referred to my baby as Jordan. It was a name I loved even before I became pregnant. Whether we had a boy or girl, his or her name would be "Jordan."

Rhonda's Note

My husband Rick and I weren't really planning to have any children. We were products of the infamous chronic family disease, Family Dysfunction-itis. Rick didn't feel very confident that he'd have what it takes to be a good dad. Although I

1

understood and supported Rick with his decision, I myself knew I wanted one child... a son. One day Rick walked into the kitchen, looked at me and said, "Okay, I'm ready." "Ready for what?" I asked. "I'm ready to be a dad," he said. Most people would make that decision (or maybe the decision makes them) and life moves forward. A family would miraculously develop and family and life, as most know it, amazingly just begins. Since Rick and I were just like most people back then, we believed it really was not rocket science.

February 10, 1992

After my workout today, I picked up a pregnancy test. I had become very tired, and my breasts were hurting longer than they usually do during my period. There was a plus sign on the tester...which meant positive for PREGNANT! OH MY GOD! Of course the first person I tried to call was Rick. He was out in the field somewhere around downtown Chicago. I paced around our home, "who can I call?" The first name that popped into my head was my good friend Joanne. I called, the phone rang, she picked up and all I could do was cry. "Jo, it's a plus, I'm pregnant!" Joanne convinced me to repeat the test to be sure. The second test had me just as overjoyed as the first one. I called Joanne back and we bounced ideas between us on how I could tell Rick...Dad. I remembered that I had kept a special newspaper clipping from the time I was a 10-year-old. The illustration had the "Love Is" couple and the caption said, "Love is telling him he's going to be a daddy." Knowing he'd first check the mail, I slipped the clipping into the pile. Rick came home and followed his routine of going straight to the mail. "Hey Rhonda...

What's this? Oh my God! You're pregnant?"

Rick's eyes filled up with tears, as he hugged and kissed me. He said, "I'm so excited!" Hey Jordan, your dad looked very happy. About an hour after the shock settled in, your dad began calling everyone. He was so cute, he would go to get something in another room and forget what he was going for. Both of our faces were beaming, because Jordan was finally beginning to make his way into this world.

February 16, 1992
This evening cards and gifts were being dropped off by our friends, your soon-to-be-family. Your future Godmother Auntie Jo, dropped off a teddy bear dressed in blue. She must believe you are a boy. Actually those are my thoughts as well.

February 18, 1992
This is our first doctor's appointment. His name is Dr. Reda and he's a very nice Italian man who's about 50 years old. He talked with me for awhile before prepping me for my exam. Dr. Reda verified that I am pregnant. On our next visit, I should be able to hear your heartbeat! What a feeling…it brings tears to my eyes, as it's hard to believe that I have a life inside of me. Dr. Reda gave me vitamins and a lot of literature to read. Jordan, this seems so over-whelming.

March 5, 1992
Everyone I talk to seems so excited for us. My workouts seem effortless.

Kevin my trainer promised I would be back in shape in no time at all since I've been bodybuilding for several years now. I'm going into my third month and I know that working out will keep both you and me healthy. I hope he's telling me the truth though. Hey, so far I feel great. Jordan, thank you for not making me sick. I love you, Mommy.

March 17, 1992
When Daddy and I heard your heart beating today I got the chills. It was so awesome. What a miracle, Daddy had a lump in his throat.

March 31, 1992
We went to your Nana and Papa's on Daddy's side. It was a birthday party for them. They were both turning 60 years old. It's a very strange feeling, because all of Daddy's relatives were there. We haven't spoken with them for over three years. This is a new beginning for all of us Jordan. I even called my father. I haven't spoken to him in eight years. The only reason I am doing this is for you. You deserve the opportunity to have these relationships.

April 18, 1992
I went to see Dr. Reda again. I weighed in at 151 pounds. I normally carry around 117 pounds. I feel huge! The doctor says your heartbeat is 160 beats per minute. The nurse reassures me that this is good. Jordan, I went to a psychic before you were a twinkle in my eye. She said I would begin to have psychic experiences while pregnant. I wasn't sure how to take that but I wasn't concerned, as I am very intuitive. But guess what? She was right. A beautiful woman who looked like an angel was sitting on the side of my bed. She was looking at me like a mother would look at her own child. I don't know who she was but she

took me by surprise. I screamed and she faded away, I wonder if she'll come back.

<u>May 13, 1992</u>

Another doctor's visit and everything seems to be normal. I have gained a total of twenty-seven pounds. I gained two pounds since the last visit. I don't think that's too bad. I'm relieved that I now look pregnant and not just chubby. Your Dad is a land-scaper and a great one at that. He works long and hard hours especially during this time of the year. So while Daddy is working a lot - I am doing most of the work on your room. I want so desperately to finish your room, but it's a slow process. Mother's Day came and went. Your cousin Michael sent a card. It's truly a strange feeling thinking soon I will be a Mommy.

<u>May 28, 1992</u>

Daddy went with me today for our first ultrasound. Again, I am moved to tears. I now understand what women mean when they talk about being so emotional during pregnancy. Or maybe it is because I saw you, sucking on your little hand. I looked up to see Daddy's reaction. Daddy was so overwhelmed by you too. Very overwhelmed…I'm not talk-ing 'teary eyed' either. I'm talking overwhelmed as in green. The color green. Yep, Daddy began to pass out slowly, slid-ing to the floor. I wonder if the staff in the delivery room will be peeling him off the floor when you are born.

Only four more months and I'll have you in my arms. I can hardly wait. By the way, Daddy ended up being okay.

<u>June 1, 1992</u>

I received the results of the ultrasound today and everything looks great. There is a concern, however. The placenta is covering the cervix. This means, if it doesn't move by your due date I will be given a Cesarean section and I will not be able to deliver naturally. At this point, it really doesn't matter, as long as you're safe. The doctors told me that this happens. I'm only hoping that medically it isn't an issue.

June 6, 1992

I'm feeling a lot of movement now. My ribs are causing me discomfort. They feel like they're crammed together, and it's awful. By the way, your Mom is a cosmetologist, Jordan. My business does really well, too. My clients have commented that I don't look six months pregnant, because my tummy still looks so small. (Good)

June 11, 1992

Dr. Reda scolded me today. He feels that I've gained too much weight since my last visit. What does he know anyway? You're hungry and I need to feed you, right? Auntie Jo is picking me up and we'll be off to register at the Babies Room. I'll be picking out your furniture and the rest of the things you'll need.

July 8, 1992

Oh my Lord, I've gained 30 pounds! I feel so fat! I am now seven months and my tummy is still on the small side. Dr. Reda is teasing me saying that I've gained the weight everywhere else except my tummy. Nice guy.

My girlfriend, Mary Jane and I went to pick out material today for your room. It's going to look so great. There will be another ultrasound in two weeks. I'm still trying to decide if I want to know your sex. I told Dr. Reda I want to make sure I get the epidural. An epidural numbs the body from the waist down during delivery. He laughed and said, "You're no fool." I'm thinking, why should I be in pain if I don't have to. I'm assured that this is safe.

September 8, 1992

I went for my second ultrasound today and I found out that you are a boy. (I knew it!) I took Nana and Grandma Linda with me so they will be part of our pregnancy. You were so active it was really exciting. You were sucking on your little toes. The nurse smiled and began chuckling. "For such a tiny baby, he's very well endowed, he's showing off already!" When Daddy came home tonight, the first thing out of his mouth was "Well honey, do you know the sex of our little one?" "Of course Jordan is a boy." I then told him what the nurse said. Daddy said, "That's my boy!" Nine more weeks, I hope.

September 15, 1992

I feel like a pig! About four more weeks, I am so uncomfortable and I'm getting a double chin! I'm beginning to get really nervous and extremely crabby. Remembering back to when I married your father, I don't recall ever having this unsettling feeling. I wonder if it's because I have loose ends. I've never been comfortable being the guest of honor at parties

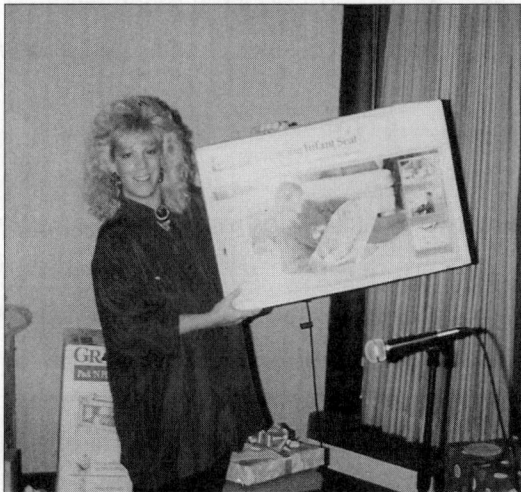

7

and we have two showers scheduled for this weekend, Nana's and the girls from the health club. Next month is Grandma Linda's party. I wish this would pass fast.

September 25, 1992

Now I'm really getting frustrated. I was hoping you'd come early. Today Dr. Reda gave me an exam which showed "bloody show." This was followed by a contraction right on the exam table. When you have your 'bloody show,' they say that the birth isn't far away. I have to tell you, Daddy and I are both very stressed out. Neither one of us has any idea what to expect.

October 3, 1992

I'm waiting Jordan. Where are you? Every time Daddy leaves the house he is worried his pager will go off. All day the phone has been ringing, everyone wants to know "Have you had the baby yet?" Everyone has also been giving a lot of unsolicited advice. "Eat Chinese, go for a bumpy ride, have great sex." (Yeah, like that's the last thing on my mind.) I'm looking out the window, and I see a full moon with lots of stars. "Star light star bright is there anyway that I could have this baby tonight?"

October 5, 1992

Well Jordan, I went to Dr. Reda today. I'm being admitted to Central DuPage Hospital at 6:30 a.m. tomorrow morning. This is it, the moment we all have been waiting for. I'll be induced with a drug called Potoesin. I'm a little concerned as I heard it's painful. I am however, liking the fact that labor won't be a sudden surprise. I'm very nervous but I am so looking forward to meeting you. You alone are worth it. See you in about 24 hours. Love, Mommy. (I like the sound of that.)

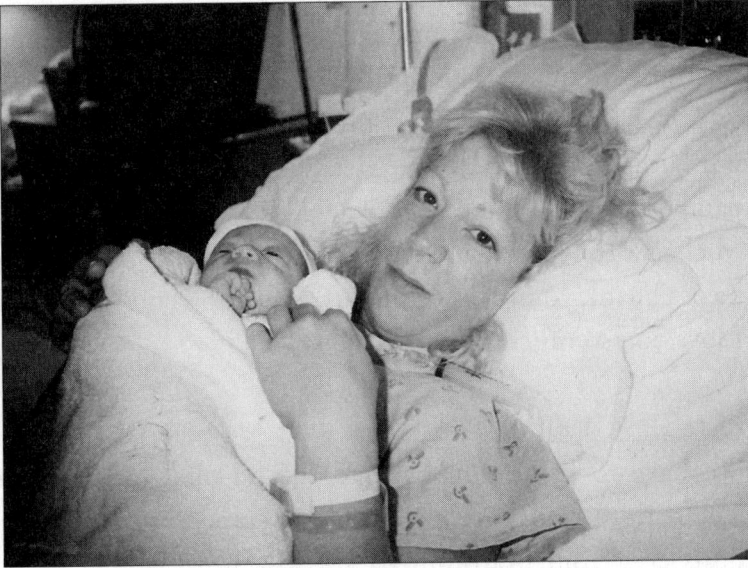

Happy Birthday, Jordan Michael Brunett—Born October 6, 1992!

Our labor was 16 1/2 hours long. I went in at 6:30 a.m. and gave birth to you at 10:53 p.m.

December 12, 1992

Jordan, I'm so sorry that I've neglected to write in your journal. You have kept me very busy and tired. You're truly a miracle! The hospital staff treated us all fantastic. I don't really remember how long into the labor I was when my water bag broke. But the next thing I remember was the pain starting. The pain began to progress slowly and I was then given the epidural, which was a good thing, since you were positioned face up.

Dr. Heitzler was the doctor on duty, and he had to turn you around. You were stuck in the birth canal and after a couple hours, Dr. Heitzler explained that if I didn't succeed with the next push, I would have to have a Cesarean section. He put a suction cup on your head and proceeded to suction you out while I pushed. It was great teamwork and the most strenuous workout I've ever had.

Dr. Heitzler laid you on my belly and Daddy cut your umbilical cord. You know, I really did forget all about the pain, just like a lot of people told me I would. Jordan Michael Brunett, you are the most beautiful baby I have ever seen. Thank you for choosing us as your parents.
I love you so much, Mommy.

October 8, 1992

We have to bring you back to the hospital today. You would think you were having major surgery, and all I can do is cry. Your billirubin count is over 20, which means your skin is a little jaundiced. A nurse puts a little band around your eyes for protection and lays you in a sun bed for 24 hours. We were assured that you will be taken good care of. The nurses on duty suggested that Daddy and I go home and get some rest. Daddy called the hospital to check on you every two or three hours. The nurses tell Daddy that you are doing great and they are enjoying your stay.

October 16, 1992 (Jordan, six weeks old)

It's been long days and nights since your hospital stay, and I can't seem to get you on a schedule. It's as though you're afraid you're going to miss something. You don't sleep much at all. After six weeks of breast-feeding, I've decided to stop. In one of the books I read it says that a baby should get everything they need for the immune system within a six-week time frame. I'm going to miss holding you close to my body. A mother just can't describe the feeling. But on the other hand I feel so tied down. You

need to be fed every
two hours, both day
and night. This is a lot
just for me to do. Now
that Daddy can help
out, I can get some
much-needed rest.

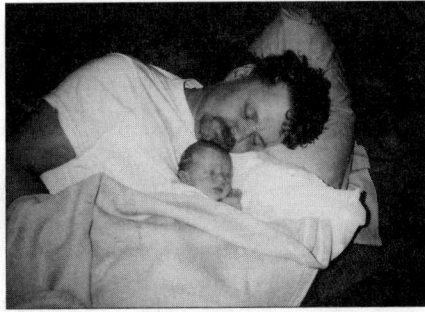

November 15, 1992
Well, you're drinking from a bottle. You are sleeping more
frequently, and I like that. Everyone has commented that
you look just like your Daddy's baby picture when he was
the same age you are now.

I've been taking you to Nana's for two hours while I go to
the health club. You seem really nervous around her, and I'm
not sure why. Maybe you sense something I don't. I love you
more than life itself. You're a good little boy, Jordan.

December 14, 1992
Jordan, you're three months old. Here are some of the new
things you are now doing: blowing bubbles, cooing, and
watching every move I make. It seems like you're growing
so fast, it's freaking me out. I want to hold you all the time,
you feel so good to me. We decided you needed a baby sitter, and her name is Kristina. She does a wonderful job with
you. I have decided to start my own business out of our
home. This is the best thing I've ever done, next to marry-
ing your father and giving birth to you. This way I'll always
be here if you should ever need me.

Dec 30, 1992
This is our first Christmas and New Year's with you and it is

very fun. Well, for us of course, since you don't have a clue. There are a lot of nice gifts and warm welcomes for your first holidays, Jordan. We went to both sides of the family and everyone enjoyed doting on you.

February 5, 1993

You are so cute, so big, and so heavy. This sounds weird but I love your cry face. I can picture it in my mind as I write this. When Daddy comes home from work you begin moving all over the place, kicking your arms and legs. I adore you.

March 22, 1993

Jordan, you found your hands! You just realized that you could control hand to mouth coordination. So all day long you are chewing on your hands. I think you should be turning over soon; it seems as though you're really trying to. Every now and then you also notice that you have feet. My girlfriend Mary Jane dropped off your Christening gown. She made it from my wedding dress. Both sets of your grandparents have gowns that have been passed down through the generations. Guess what? We are starting our own family tradition. Jordan, if you choose not to carry it on that's okay with me. Your baptism is on April 13th and your Godparents are your cousin Mike and my life long friend Joanne.

Excerpt Godfather Mike

Right after Jordan was born, I was asked to be his Godfather. I was honored and gladly accepted. This was well before we knew how special Jordan is. I also had the opportunity to live with and help raise Jordan for almost four years while living with Rick and Rhonda. I moved into Jordan's home right after his first birthday.

He was already well into his alphabets, shapes, colors, and presidential flashcards. This time for him was just incredible. He would sit and focus so strongly on each and every one of those flashcards. To all of us this was cute; however, we had no idea that at 18 months he was not only focusing on each card but he was engraving each one in that little mind of his. As he grew older he got into routines. The difficult part for everyone was keeping to these routines. You see, a broken routine to Jordan made everyone who was involved in Jordan's day difficult, including Jordan.

Excerpt Godmother JoJo

Wow! That was the first thing I said, thought and felt the first time I held you and looked into your eyes. I told your mom that I couldn't explain it but you were going to grow up and be someone amazing. As you were growing into a toddler, I saw a different kind of a toddler. Something in your eyes was so intense. It seemed that when you looked at something, you locked onto it as if you were trying to immerse yourself into it.

May 22, 1993

Wow, everyday you're changing. The latest is your two bottom teeth. Of course with teeth coming in, there are mood swings. You're allowed to have Tylenol every four hours, it helps.

July 1, 1993

Jordan you said "Dada" for the first time. Daddy thinks I should keep track of all your firsts. That's a little too much, but I will try. Earlier today when I was in the Jewel grocery store I was amazed that you started waving at the checkout woman. What a little flirt you are. I didn't teach you that, but Daddy always waves at you so I guess you finally decided to put those hands to good use. You're so cute.

July 25, 1993

You're crawling, oh my God! I'd say you are Hell on wheels. There are a couple of things I want to tell you. Things like, when I feed you in your highchair inbetween bites you roll your fingers like you're bored. You gave my girlfriend's baby daughter, Jenna an open mouth kiss. You crawled up to her, stopped, opened your mouth and planted one right on her lips. The funny part is you went on your merry old way right after that. Pat and I were laughing hysterically. Oh yeah, you have added more to your vocabulary. Dada, kitty, baba, and doggie. I am reading flash cards of the presidents. It entertains you.

2

Mommy and Jordan Time, All the Time

<u>August 18, 1993</u>

My gosh! Jordan, you are getting so big and very active. I'm getting incredibly tired. Your first summer has been busy. We are lucky. Daddy has managed to get some time off from work. We have been having some great fun together as a family. So far we have taken you to an amusement park called Santa's Village.

I don't know who had more fun, Daddy or you? We also spent the afternoon at the Chicago Cub's baseball park. You actually sat pretty well until the last inning. This is pretty understandable since it was a long day for a baby. Some new things you're doing: crawling and standing with the help of furniture. And Jordan, guess what? You began crawling up the stairs today! I also have noticed that since you've turned 10 months old, all my help has vanished! Family members have disappeared. I do have two wonderful babysitters, though, without whom I would be very lost.

September 1, 1993

Jordan, you are really killing me. You are so active; my Lord help me. This job of Motherhood is the hardest work I have ever had. You're definitely worth it, but nobody prepares you for this sort of thing. I really feel a mother's job is overlooked. Women just don't get the credit they deserve. A man's physical labor can't even compare to the twenty-four hour a day job of motherhood.

Don't get me wrong, I love it and you're the best thing that ever happened to me, but I never imagined the energy you would have.

October 6, 1993

Happy Birthday to you, Happy Birthday to you, Happy Birthday, Dear Jordan, Happy Birthday to you. Happy Birthday, Jordan, you are now one-year-old. Love, Mommy.

I videotaped your birthday party and as far as talking goes, you're still saying Dada, doggie, and hi. You're getting pretty brave and managing to take a couple of steps. You don't sleep through the night and I'm up at least twice a night to check on you. You love to crawl all over the place. Peek-a-boo and hide-and-seek give you big belly laughs. Daddy can get you really laughing. When he throws you on the couch he'll say "take that, and that, and that." You laugh so hard it's contagious. I'm considering finding someone to watch you when I go to the health club. You cry at Nana's for 30 minutes out of the hour while I am gone. I can't stand to see you so upset. I can't help but wonder why you do that.

Excerpt Neighbor Laura

I first met Jordan when he was going to soon be a one-year-old. I remember Rhonda doing flash cards of presidents with Jordan. They would go through the whole pack over and over, one at a time, three times a day. This amazingly seemed to keep his attention.

October 20, 1993

We are still playing with the president flashcards. You seem to still really like it. Jordan, you have an Aunt Sue, who has Cerebral Palsy and a rare form of Epilepsy. I remember my mom (your grandma Linda) doing all she could do to keep Sue's mind stimulated. I figure, why not stimulate your little mind? We spend 24 hours together so we might as well both be learning. I videotaped us doing this to show you when you get big.

November 6, 1993

I recently wrote a letter to basketball superstar, Michael Jordan. He retired on October 6, 1993, which is your birthday. I wanted to tell him how amazing I thought it was that you're his namesake, plus he retired on your birthday. I THINK IT'S PRETTY COOL. I know every mom has hopes of their children accomplishing something of importance in their lifetime. Whatever it is that you accomplish, it will be in a grand way. I feel it in my bones. I hope that by being one of your teachers I am able to direct you down your chosen path. I believe that God speaks through other people. I pay very close attention to what I hear and I go with it. Well, onto the things you are doing at this time. You took five steps and then you fell. You have four teeth on the bottom and four on the top. Your eyes have a sparkle that is almost an angelic gleam. People have told me that they can't help but stare at you because you are so cute.

December 1, 1993

Jordan, you're now walking all over the place. I am so very tired. I literally chase after you all day long. You're an expert stair climber and very fast! You're also very aware of everything this holiday. At 14 months old, Jordan, you have taken a great interest in your learning toys, especially numbers and lettered blocks. I am pretty active myself and I can't believe how you wipe me out. You never seem to tire as you go all over.

January 1, 1994

First year molars and the teeth directly in front of them on top are in. You're not very happy about that. You are still into Barney the Dinosaur—big time. Daddy and I were watching TV on the floor and you crawled over and gave me a big kiss. It was so sweet, you almost made us cry. You've become so funny. I'm beginning to think acting is something you should consider.

You put a big smile on my face. Just recently you had your shots for mumps, measles, and rubella. I think that's what they're called. You're extremely cranky getting the shots and your molars in at the same time.

3

You and Your Environment: Mimicking and Anti-Social

<u>March 6, 1994</u>

Your newest thing is twirling in circles. You've cut almost all of your teeth.

You have a farm animal book that is your favorite toy. You make all the sounds. The frog goes croak, the cow goes moo, and you mimic these words after I read them. You are so smart.

<u>April 5, 1994</u>

I took you for your first professional picture today. I have a feeling your molars are really bothering you. You didn't do well at all. Finally the photographer sang, "Pop goes the Weasel" and popped his head from behind the curtain, and then you calmed down and relaxed. The man was able to get quite a few decent shots. Things you're now doing; you still like the farm book and you've added the

Crow's Caw. You shift your eyes to the right and do a deep knee bend to the song Sally the Camel that's on your Barney tape. While viewing the videotape you mimic the children. I have you involved at the Park District in a program for tots. You go off and play by yourself. I can't get you to sit in a circle with the others. It's like you have your own agenda.

Excerpt Friend Janet

I will never forget the overwhelming sense that I had about the child Rhonda was carrying and how special he was going to be. When Jordan was born, that was the closest I had ever consistently been around an infant. I had no idea what "normal" for an infant was, and each thing he did seemed so spectacularly intelligent and incredible. I remember being amazed at the attention he could give, even at a young age, to Barney. I remember holding him and feeling the baby I was carrying (Justin) kicking inside me as if to say "Hey, Mom!! Let me out! That's my buddy you're holding and I want to come out and play." When Justin did "come out and play," that started a whole new dimension to the relationship Rhonda and I had as friends, and to the dimension of infant observation we were having, i.e. Jordan and Justin as individuals, as "buddies," etc. As excited as I was to see Justin's developmental progress, I was beginning to become devastated to see the contrast between his and Jordan's development.

April 6, 1994 (Jordan, 18 Months)

Easter was a nice holiday this year. You were wired for sound. We went out for Easter brunch with Grandma Linda and Sue.

For some reason you were extremely cranky. A couple of days before this we went to see the Easter Bunny, and you ran up to him and hugged him like he was only there for you.

April 16, 1994

You speak what sounds like Japanese. It's so funny, over and over you say "hi," but you say the "I" like an "E" dragging it out. You're still crabby, but your molars are trying to come through. I got my first dirty look from you today.

You kept throwing your bottle. I explained to you that if you threw it again, I was going to take it away from you. Well, you threw it. And I had to take it away from you. Your eyes opened really wide, you glared at me, turned, and walked away.

It was so funny that Dad and I had to laugh.

May 10, 1994

Today you got your first black eye. I dressed you and we were all ready to go to Brookfield Zoo. We were waiting for Grandma Edie, when you went darting across the room tripping over your own feet. You hit the toy box (ouch!).

Jordan, you have cuts and bruises all over you. Our day at the zoo was fabulous. There seemed to be no problems as far as you were concerned. Your newest thing is running and looking back at your shadow. It's hilarious! You'll go around the block three times continuously and keep looking behind at your shadow.

Hey, there was a Solar Eclipse from noon until one. This won't happen again until the year 2009. The second newsworthy event that occurred was the execution of John Wayne Gacey. He was convicted of killing many boys and men. You can look up his story when you get big if you want to. It's too sad and sick to put into your journal.

May 28, 1994

We were lying in our bed and you looked at your mom and dad when your very first sentence came out of your mouth. You said, "I love you" and later on you said "oh oh." You're so smart.

June 25, 1994

Man, you have another double ear infection. What's with that? My Lord, it also seems like you drool in lakes. You're still talking Japanese and trying to walk up and down the stairs on your own. It scares the crap out of me. Sweet, oh are you sweet! Still crabby, but sweet!

July 4, 1994

Oh Jordan, you love the outdoors. We went by Auntie's for a Fourth of July party. You walked up and down the streets. I'm amazed you went swimming, picked up a basketball, and you tried to make a basket. Wow, and only 21 months old! The fireworks didn't seem to effect you.

Excerpt Grandma Linda

When my grandson was born, I honestly never noticed anything unusual about him. I'm positive I would have too, because my youngest child was born with Cerebral Palsy and a rare form of epilepsy and I was looking for symptoms.

I was very happy to see none. Unfortunately, I wasn't around a lot to really observe Jordan's activities, but on one occasion I do remember at a family party being able to do this. Jordan was constantly running around the room looking at the chairs and the furniture from all angles. Deep down I knew something wasn't right. My sister noticed it also and asked me about it. I know we were both concerned, but unsure why. Another time while Rhonda was doing my hair, she placed Jordan on my lap. He started screaming and wouldn't stop. His actions startled me and my daughter became very upset.

July 5, 1994

You're in a great mood today. We went to the park, came home, and took a nap. We went to McDonalds for lunch and we split a cheeseburger and fries. Then later we went swimming by Aunt Linda's. This is one of those perfect days. Grandma Linda stopped by and she brought you some sort of cute soccer cap.

Excerpt Neighbor Marian

The first time I saw Jordan, he was running down the street at 25 mph with his mom trying to keep up with him. When I met them, his mom couldn't keep a lengthy conversation because Jordan couldn't stay in one spot for long without wanting to run. The neighborhood kids found him hard to play with. Jordan didn't make a lot of eye contact. He wouldn't communicate with the kids. He seemed to prefer to play on his own.

July 9, 1994

Everyday we walk around the block at least seven times. Whoever is out at the time says hello to you. All the children seem to really love you, even the adults find you fascinating. Usually when we go for our walks, I'll point to various things and tell you what they are. I also spell them for you. On this day you wanted to bring your teddy bear. We call him your "Jordan bear." You wrapped your arms around his neck. It's so cute because the bear is just about your size. As we walked you started to point to the trees and cars, like I do. You were talking away in your Japanese. You are really so cute.

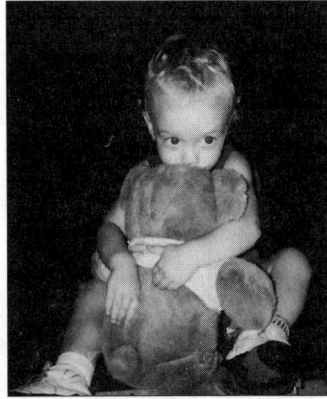

Excerpt Neighbor Carla

As Jordan's old across the street neighbor, I have known him since he was one. Jordan was always just Jordan to me. Oh sure he was a unique little guy with his own quirks. I watched him run around, and around, and around the block with Rhonda not far behind. I was at a birthday party held at our local Chuck E. Cheese. Jordan spent most of that party pacing around the tables in the pizza party area, looking as if he were counting each and every chair, while the other partygoers were sitting down enjoying treats and being entertained.

I spent several summer afternoons lounging with neighbor friends as we watched our kids develop relationships with each other through play. Rhonda tried to keep up with Jordan, who seemed to always be on the move and always only interested in doing his own thing. Jordan did do things differently, but hey, I had a son who during his stroller rides insisted on bending over and watching the wheel of the stroller rotate, instead of observing the world around him. I have always been very tolerant of people's differences and uniqueness, so at first I didn't think a thing about Jordan's behavior.

In fact, I was much more concerned about Rhonda. I didn't hang out with her on a daily basis, but she always seemed so nervous and uptight whenever we were at birthday parties or play dates together. She apologized for Jordan's behavior over and over and usually was the first to leave any gathering.

She got so frustrated about not being able to communicate with Jordan.

Rhonda shared with me that she had been drilling Jordan with flashcards daily since he was an infant. I admit, I wondered to myself if that repetitive action had contributed somehow to wiring Jordan's brain for the compulsive, repetitive motions he was carrying out as a toddler (e.g. running endlessly around the block).

I later learned that Rhonda was intuitively doing exactly what she should have been to stimulate Jordan's brain development. After speaking to our neighbor Laura about Rhonda's challenges with Jordan we began to discuss the possibility of autism. Neither of us really had much information.

One day I was trying to play with Jordan with one of those Disney Pop Up toys. You would hit one of the colored buttons and a Disney character pops up out of a hole to reward you. No matter how many different ways I tried, Jordan couldn't get the cause and effect relationship. I would push a red button and Mickey would jump up to greet me. When it was Jordan's turn, he would always go back to the red hole that Mickey jumped out of and try to pry it open to get Mickey to come out. I shared the information with

Rhonda and she borrowed the toy to work with Jordan. Eventually she was able to train Jordan to push the buttons, but at his age he should have been able to do it automatically. Perhaps there was something more to Jordan's differences than I thought. It wasn't until I tried playing with Jordan that I realized I would have to offer unsolicited advice.

Not an easy thing for someone who doesn't give her opinions unless asked.

Definition of autism provided by A.D.A.M. INC.
Autism is a complex developmental disorder that appears in the first 3 years of life, though it is sometimes diagnosed much later. It affects the brain's normal development of social and communication skills.

Autism is a spectrum that encompasses a wide continuum of behavior. Core features include impaired social interactions, impaired verbal and non verbal communication and restricted and repetitive patterns of behavior.

Symptoms may vary from quite mild to quite severe. Mild autism is known as Asperger's syndrome.

July 10, 1994

I went to an Astrologer today. She confirmed everything I already knew. She said you're a very lucky child. Mommy and Daddy's purpose is to teach you all about love. One day many people will be listening to what you have to say. This will be on a very large scale. You will be a wealthy man and will make right what is wrong with the world. I am so blessed to have you for my son. Jordan means descending and Michael means from God. Thank you for coming Jordan.

July 29, 1994

You are always telling Daddy that you love him. I have to admit I'm a bit jealous because I'm the one who spends every second with you.

A couple of days ago, I took you to a friend's house and they had a little tyke activity center. You had a blast on this! Daddy loves you so much, that he went out that evening and bought you your own Little Tyke activity center. Just a little spoiled?

August 16, 1994

You're jabbering away. When you do something, whether playing or trying to talk, you seem very focused and determined. I took you for a walk the other day.

You walked up to a car in a driveway and kept circling it. You were walking around and around and around. You had to have gone around at least six times. I wanted to continue walking. You on the other hand weren't going anywhere. I tried picking you up and you squeezed down on your arms so I couldn't lift you. I then picked you up and carried you four or five houses away. As soon as I put you down, you ran right back to the house we came from and continued to circle the car. Oh well.

Excerpt Friend Janet

I recall how Jordan would seem completely immersed in things like the wheels on cars. He would just run around and around the car, analyzing the tires. He would tirelessly repeat the same path around the car as if he saw something completely new and exciting each time. I also remember the joy that Rhonda felt the first time he looked up in the sky and saw an airplane.

HE LOOKED UP!!!

He had realized that there was so much more to his world than what he could see by looking down. I also remember Jordan holding objects, any object, and analyzing every angle that it had over and over. Again, tireless repetition. It was almost as if he could see something that no one else could.

September 1, 1994

Hello Jordan, my little angel baby. Well, today I feel worn out and by the end of the day, I'm toast. What are you doing now? You smack your lips together when I ask you for a kiss. You play Patty Cake and Itsy Bitsy Spider. You wink in the mirror, and you say "Oh" and "Bye-Bye." You do that very well. Another thing you're doing is starting to throw tantrums. You have a very strong will. You definitely capture people's attention, that's for sure. Crabby today, those second year molars could be why.

Daddy's dog Misty had a stroke. It's so sad, it seems like Daddy's been giving you extra hugs and kisses. I think it brings him a little comfort. You call Misty, "Auggie." We have an extended family with our neighbors. They are from India and they tell me that you're speaking Eastern Indian. All your gibbering, at least someone can understand what you're saying. I wonder if you were from India in your last life.

September 14, 1994

You are into everything! When I go to change your diaper you take off running. Barney the Dinosaur's video has one song that is so cute. They sing "The ants go marching one by one, hurrah, hurrah." You mouth the words and throw your arms up in the air. I'll ask you "Hey little boy, how old are you?" and you respond "two." Another ear infection; this has you so crabby and I can't blame you. I'm beginning to realize that you're having a lot of ear infections. I'm concerned about what the effects of the antibiotics might be doing to you. Cousin Mike lives with us; you look forward to him coming home. Both of you wrestle, Mike will contort you into all these different moves and you think it's great. It's no sooner than one minute that he walks through the door and it's time to be thrown around. Usually before bed you have ice cream as a treat with Daddy.

<u>September 22, 1994</u>
You can say "baseball" but not "Mommy." I wonder why?

Excerpt Friend Janet

Up until Jordan was nearly two, when he would want something—a drink, a snack, a toy, whatever—he would not say what he wanted. He just made a sound or a gesture that only Rhonda, as his mom, knew. His form of communication was so different from what I had grown accustomed to with Justin. The other thing that comes to mind is how Jordan almost seemed pained if someone hugged him and wanted absolutely NO human touch. He didn't want to be held, rocked or have a kiss on the cheek. Rhonda was actually working with him on this. She had started some play therapy, which involved doing touchy things like touching his face, brushing his hair, etc. Although I knew that one child is different from another, I began to realize the differences in Jordan's development.

Excerpt Friend Terry

Looking back, I can remember the first time I met Rhonda and Jordan. We were at the park in Bloomingdale. I was with my son, Jeremy, and Rhonda was with Jordan. Jordan and Jeremy were one year apart. Jeremy was three and Jordan was two. Jeremy was running around checking everything out that he could. Jeremy would climb the slide, dig in the sand and swing on the swings. He did this totally oblivious of me or anyone else. Jordan, on the other hand, would not leave Rhonda's side. Jordan wouldn't even climb the slide unless Rhonda was right there with him. She would place him on her lap and slide down with him. Jordan did, however, enjoy the park.

October 6, 1994 (Jordan, two years old)

Jordan you are two years old now. Goodness we had a fabulous day. We went to the park and played there for awhile. When you got up from your nap, we walked around the block a few times then went to McDonalds for lunch. We later had cake at home and out again for a free Baskin & Robbins birthday cone. Later that evening Auntie JoJo dropped by with a birthday gift. It's a remote control car-pretty cool. Jill, your babysitter, stopped over to wish you a happy birthday and lots of calls from relatives continuously came in. You are a very lucky boy and I'm a very lucky Mom.

October 22, 1994

Boy, are you independent! We bought you a toddler bed, and you discovered how to get out of it. I wake up to find you in bed with us. It happens a lot. When it's bedtime you run around like a wild man screaming and yelling. You will perform a lot of itsy bitsy spiders, the ants go marching, and flying in an airplane. You also love to look into the mirror. Sleep, however, you fight tooth and nail!

October 25, 1994

It is fall now and you love the leaves. You can spend hours, and this is no joke, throwing the leaves into the air. I forgot to tell you about your second birthday! We hired Lollipop the Clown. All the children were wonderful, but you weren't so keen to be around all the kids. Lollipop performed for about an hour and thirty minutes; we opened gifts and had cake. Yummy! Personally, the cake was my favorite part. Later that evening we had Grandparents and the rest of the family over. You and Aunt Sue shared your birthday cake and you put the candle out with your finger-ouch!*
I love you, Jordan, Happy Birthday.

*When we review his birthday tape, we can see that although Jordan does put the candle out with his finger, it is almost like he had a delayed reaction to the pain of being burnt.

Excerpt Friend Cindy

I think back to the time when Jordan and Rhonda were a weekly part of my life. I am a Special Education teacher and had taught for 10 years before staying home and being part of this special group of people. When I started socializing with everyone Jordan was a 2-year-old boy. The thing I noticed about him was that he did not interact socially. He would be in his own world. Jordan marched to a different drummer and did not seem to be aware of much that was happening outside of him. We accepted this as a group. We had a collective philosophy that cherished each individual child. It was a child-centered environment with lots of love and acceptance. Rhonda was a stressed parent. Where the other children were growing past the phase where we had to chase behind them and could enjoy different experiences, Jordan continued to require constant vigilance. Jordan would walk out and leave the house. He had episodes when he was completely over stimulated and couldn't take any more. He had ritual behaviors. I was concerned most about the lack of appropriate social development. Both my sister Laura and our friend, Carla began to express concerns. Rhonda would sometimes tear up when we'd get together. Jordan would not participate in the fun activities.

We spoke often that Jordan should be evaluated at the School District. We just weren't sure with Rhonda's state of mind how to approach it.

October 31, 1994

Halloween and we dressed you up as Barney the Dinosaur. You refused to wear your mask. We went to a few friends and family homes. You received money, bubbles, and lots of candy.

December 1, 1994

Life is moving so quickly, or should I include you in that as well? Lately you mumble a lot of gibberish. There are words that come out every so often. Yesterday, Daddy gave you a cookie and you said "thank you."

Daddy had friends over watching the football game. During a play Barney yelled, "Yeah baby!" and you repeated it. Oh, I almost forgot, you also said "Q, R, S, T, U, V;" I said, "What did you say, Jordan?"

I wish you would start talking. It's been two years of a one sided conversation and, quite frankly, I'm getting tired of doing all the talking.

December 28, 1994
Today when Daddy came home from work, he asked for a big hug. On a normal day you're engrossed in your playing and would ignore him. Not today though. You turned and with your little arms stretched open wide you ran into his arms. All I have to say is, some things are worth waiting for.

January 28, 1995
You are so funny; your latest thing is walking around with your eyes closed. You crinkle your nose and make this silly face. The mirror is still your friend; you are still singing into the mirror and dancing to your Barney tapes.

You've also taken a liking to Matchbox cars; however, you're not playing with them. You line them up and study each car at great length. Your favorite toy is the United States of America puzzle. You take each piece one by one and, holding it level with your nose, you swing it level to your ear and then set it on top of the table. You will do this same routine with each and every piece of the puzzle, just like the Matchbox cars.

I can't help but wonder, Jordan, what you were doing? We took you to see Santa. You didn't care much for the man! As a matter of fact you could care less about Christmas. I wonder if you will enjoy your gifts. Let's see, some of the things you are doing now: you are doing your alphabet. You recognize letters, but sometimes you get M and W confused. I think it has a lot to do with the fact that these letters are the same color.

February 3, 1995 (Jordan, 28 months)

Oh my, you are starting to talk up a storm! Well, anything is better then nothing at all! You sing E.I.E.I.O., from Old Macdonald. Then you go into animal sounds. You have a book of sounds: the cow goes moo, and the horse goes nay. Ring around the Rosy is also popular these days. Oh, guess what? I told you that I loved you today and you said it back. Keep it up and I'll give you the world. I'm noticing that you're saying words and singing but not conversing. For instance, you haven't said, "Mommy, I want a cookie."

March 8, 1995

Something tells me you are Albert Einstein material. You are so smart. You know how to read and you know things by heart! If I repeat myself in this journal, Jordan, I'm sorry. Sometimes I can't remember if I told you every-thing. You're starting to color. I tried holding off on this because you would eat the crayons or at least try to. A virus has been going around and you have been sick for three weeks. You have a croup cough and I'm starting to go a little stir crazy. Tomorrow's my birthday, Jordan. I will be 34 years old. This is going to be my lucky year. I'm already lucky though, because I have you.

XO Mommy.

Rhonda's Note
Although we had wonderful times and my son filled my life with joy, there were plenty of not so wonderful times. In hind-sight, as I will mention repeatedly, I did have a support system,

but when you're in the mix, you're not aware and just can't seem to see or feel them. All you feel is alone. It's hard for the average person to understand what it's like to raise an autistic child. Imagine for a moment that you had a child from another land who doesn't speak your language and you had to teach that child to communicate with society and act appropriately in

*social settings. **Imagine this child fights you tooth and nail, with high-pitched screams and possible physical attacks.** This is the best way I can explain to you my feelings of isolation amidst my amazing support system.*

Excerpt Neighborhood "Grandma" Hilda

I've known Jordan since the age of two. When I was new to the neighborhood, I would get very upset when I would watch Jordan's mother carry him horseback all around her yard. I couldn't understand why she did this. One day I asked her and she explained that if she would put him down he would run non-stop around the block. Carrying him horseback was how Rhonda would get a break.

March 14, 1995

Well, we're back to our old routine. You run around the block ten times a day. You were pushing children at the park today as though you owned it! It seems that you're having a hard time with the concept of sharing, I think that's normal. Janet and Justin were over for dinner. You turned to him and babbled something and he just gave you this puzzled look. Justin is a 2-year-old boy and he talks in sentences. The funny part was that his response to you was "blah, blah, blah." Janet and I started cracking up laughing, it was so funny, and I almost peed my pants. Easter was cool, you still don't quite understand, but you did have fun. Your Nana had an Easter egg hunt with a lot of candy and loose change.

April 21, 1995

You are still singing a lot lately from your Barney tapes. You especially repeat these songs: Twinkle, Twinkle, Little Star, She'll Be Coming Around the Mountain, and Six Little Ducks. You love bubbles and have been known to play with them for an hour straight. You are still talking gibberish. Swati, our little Indian girlfriend, said you must be reincarnated. In your last life you must have been an Indian rock star. You're babbling sounds like Eastern Indian and you love to sing. It's so cute. You are still running around the block 10 times a day.

May 25, 1995

You love to jump on the couch. Daddy and you have this

game where he says "One, two, three, fall!" You laugh a lot when you two do this, and you now mimic Daddy's expressions. You open your eyes really wide waiting for him to say, "FALL!" You're still not talking very much.

I notice that when the children come over to play with you, you are very independent and prefer to play alone than with them.

June 11, 1995

Daddy brought home a cute little house. You played for two hours in it! I peek into the windows and say, "I see you" and you repeat back to me, "I see you."

On a daily basis you are counting to 10. I'm so proud of you.

June 17, 1995

Daddy was chasing you down the street the other day. He was yelling, "Stop Jordan! I'm not going around the block with you right now." As clear as a bell you said, "I don't like you" and Daddy said back to you, "but I love you." It's pretty funny; Daddy turned to me and said, "I'm so hurt." Twenty is the lucky number this week. You're counting to twenty. You say, "Yow baby" and "bye-bye." I keep thinking you're going to start talking any time now!

4

Is It Me, Or Is It You? Where to Begin Prescreening?

Excerpt Friend Edie

It was at this point that Rhonda started to worry that there might be something not quite right with Jordan. While his brightness was never in question, he displayed certain characteristics that were different than others his age and as Rhonda's "older and wiser" friend, I would reassure her that all children progress at their own level. Probably the most noticeable of these characteristics was his lack of interest in speaking, his intense examination of things, and his disinterest in showing any physical affection to anyone other then his parents.

<u>July 4, 1995</u>

Here are some new things to add to your list of phrases. "Shut up, Put me down, I love you, and Ring around the Rosy." Screaming tantrums have begun. It's driving me crazy. You seem to be very unreasonable at times. I guess that's why they call it the terrible twos. Man, talk about me getting wound up like a top, these tantrums hit every nerve in my body. We've been real busy lately going to the zoo, different parks, carnivals, bike rides with me as the driver of course. I love you, Jordan, and I hope we can do things together forever.

Excerpt Neighbor Carla

Several weeks after my interaction with and closer observation of Jordan, I was watching "Good Morning America" when they showed a segment on autism.

I listened intently and what was being described did resemble some of Jordan's characteristics and behaviors, but in very general terms. The message the parents were sending out however, was very clear. **Early diagnosis and intervention is so very important and had contributed significantly to their child's high level of functioning.** As fate would have it, Rhonda was having a particularly challenging time with Jordan and she was going quite crazy. I persuaded her to leave him with me for a half-hour or so and take a break. Jordan didn't play with my son. He did keep himself entertained for awhile and didn't start pacing until it was almost time for her to return. When Rhonda did return she poured out the frustrations and challenges of parenting. She ended our conversation with, "I don't know what I'm supposed to do." I took this as permission from her to voice my opinion. I told her to take advantage of our school district's free preschool screening program for Jordan. By the next day she had the number and was setting up the screening.

Rhonda's Note

At this point in time, I was a wreck. I couldn't control my son and I felt like a complete failure when it came to motherhood. I couldn't even take Jordan to the store without coming unglued

I decided to take Jordan to a preschool screening based on my neighbor Carla's urging. Although many of my family members and friends were also beginning to bring pre-screening suggestion to my attention, when Carla brought it up, the timing was right.

Parents who are concerned that their children might have developmental concerns may be able to bring their child to their school district for testing. Many offer a no-cost screening. Our District #93 in Illinois is open to children up to 33 months old for screening.

As I've learned, early intervention is extremely vital—in fact, it is key!

Jordan was a few weeks short of three years old when I scheduled his screening. The person conducting the test, following guidelines, wasn't able to administer the pre-school test until he turned three. I was so frustrated that I began crying and basically begged her to help me. As a result, she scheduled the testing.

The results of that pre screening: at age three, Jordan tested to only be at 18 months developmentally. After Christmas break, he was accepted into The Preschool Special Education Program. I am so grateful to Carla and glad that I listened and acted on her advice.

Excerpt Cousin Linda

Jordan, you were hard to reach sometimes, but you would always seem to smile at me, so I assumed that you understood my presence. I felt your frustrations of trying to communicate between the ages of one and three. One day I read an article on autism in a magazine. A doctor did some sort of noise level test to the child. He discovered certain levels of noise annoyed the child. I also noticed your response and you were very much disturbed by loud noises and uncomfortable with too much activity around you. This would stress you out.

I clipped out this article and decided to mail it to your mom.

July 21, 1995

You are so affectionate lately and you are starting to become potty trained. I bought you Pull-ups and a Potty book. I'll read it and at the end of the book it says "I'm not a baby anymore, no more diapers for me, I wear real underpants now." You get really excited when we get to that part of the book. You seem to study this book. You look carefully at the children wearing underpants. I'm hoping to have you potty trained by three. That is when I plan to put real underwear on you. It's so funny—you look at the book, then at your underwear, then at the book. What fun you are, Jordan.

August 14, 1995

What an action-packed week. Terry was in from Arizona with her children Jason and Brittany. They are 13 and six years old. I took them bowling and while they bowled I chased you up and down the lanes. You were picking up other people's bowling balls and trying to throw them down the lanes. I was having heart attacks! Yesterday we were invited to Ankur's birthday. I was sitting at the kitchen table with a woman trying to be polite and make conversation when you disappeared. You walked out of the house and ran around the block heading home. When I found you, I was just sick. My girlfriend Terry is a preschool teacher. She was watching how you observe everything. She believes you could be gifted. It would be nice to be smart. I was not book smart at all, so to have a child who is book smart seems God blessed.

September 4, 1995

Well, I started you in church finally. Once we arrived we were fine. Class was from 10:30 a.m. until 12:00 p.m. When I walked in you were passing different color crayons past your eyes, sitting by yourself. I keep wondering what is going on inside your head. Well September 11th I will be taking you to a preschool screening, so shortly we will know more.

Excerpt Principal Miss Cathy

All that child needs is some limits!

That was the conclusion I drew after watching the home video of a 3-year-old who was being evaluated by our Special Services Team. In my 14 years of special education experience I had only minimal interaction with Autistic children. Pervasive Developmental Disorder/Autism was a recent diagnosis and one that carried many unanswered questions and misconceptions. My experience told me that setting attainable expectations within boundaries assisted special needs children with behavioral challenges. I have since learned that my initial reaction was based on lack of information about a very complicated disorder. Luckily, there were district personnel who recognized Jordan's need and addressed it through early intervention. I would not meet Jordan again until the fall of 1999 when he entered Elsie Johnson School as a first grader. It can only be imagined the challenges that school posed for Jordan and the challenges that Jordan posed for the regular education staff that welcomed and embraced him.

As I reflect back onto the videotape of that little boy, I did not fully understand. I hear ignorant words. Too often we apply old paradigms to unfamiliar and new situations; then we realize we made erroneous assumptions and judgments. Applying the principles of successful schools—knowledge and information, teacher support, open communication and a culture of acceptance—fosters success for any child. I have learned a lot about autism in the past years and realize that I still have a long way to go before I can ever truly appreciate the gift that Jordan's presence was at Elsie Johnson School.

Excerpt Friend Nancy

I remember when Jordan was a toddler and I knew something didn't seem quite right. But I didn't know what. I too am a mother of a special needs child and I saw things that concerned me. I recommended that Rhonda have Jordan tested at the Early Childhood Preschool Screening and I am so very thankful that she did. I believe that it made a difference.

5

The Gathering of Forces

Rhonda's Note

My younger sister is mentally challenged and has been troubled with several other illnesses, so of course my childhood was geared around her. Everyday, my mother had a house full of people providing therapy 15 hours a day for eight years. When I received Jordan's diagnosis, my reaction was "WHY GOD? WHY WOULD YOU DO THIS TO ME AGAIN?" And that is exactly how I felt and how I reacted. Rick, however, did not appear to be effected at all and was shocked by my reaction. Thank goodness that he was so grounded.

Actually the preschool speech teacher suggested that we also go to a neurologist and have Jordan tested for PDD (Pervasive Developmental Disorder), which she explained fell under the umbrella of autism. A true and specific diagnosis was the only way he would receive the help in school that he needed in order to progress.

October 1, 1995
We were supposed to go by Grandma Linda. She was going to have a party for Sue. I had to cancel! Grandma was here yesterday and you told her to go away. She looked down at you and said, "Go away?" I put you in a time out and explained that was not appropriate. You were screaming bloody murder.

Grandma said, "Give him a swat on the behind. That child is going to end up out of control!" I went off on her. She didn't like it and stormed out of the house. I'm not going to hit you. That doesn't solve anything; hitting creates hitting back, and that's not good. Daddy and I are really trying hard with you, Jordan. We want you to grow up where you are safe and loved. I don't know what to do with you. Your meltdowns are becoming quite hard, Jordan. I'm not saying that children should never get a swat on the butt. In certain situations it may be the correct response.

I just don't want it to be that whenever WE become frustrated, we resort to hitting.

October 3, 1995
Grandma Edie watched you for Daddy and me. She seems to understand you and me right now. I find it strange that you really aren't bonding with your natural grandparents when they're around. This week I'm considering buying a membership to the Children's Museum. You seem to love the atmosphere. I also brought you some Discovery Toys, and you seem to like all the books.

October 6, 1995 (Jordan, 3 years old)
You are so silly today. You put on my glasses and you were dancing around making faces to try and make Daddy and

me laugh. We went on a family outing to Goeberts Pumpkin Farm. You went into the haunted house. They had pony rides, which you absolutely loved. I think we bought the largest pumpkin Goeberts had! We gave you a party for your birthday and we invited all the neighborhood children. You played and we had cupcakes. It was a fun time.

Excerpt Jordan's Friend Swati

Early morning Jordan would come peek his head in my house and walk right in. He'd watch television with my brother until I would wake up. Then he'd ask me "Swati, will you play 500 with me?" No matter how tired I was I could not refuse Jordan's sweet little face. Every day during the summer, I would be at Jordan's house or he would be at mine. We would always find something entertaining to do. Rhonda would take us to Chuck E. Cheese, to the zoo, petting zoos and carnivals. There were so many new experiences that we first experienced together that I would never be able to forget.

Excerpt Jordan's Friend Mili

Jordan is a name we will never forget in our household. Jordan was another grandson to my grandpa, another son to my parents and another brother to my brother and sister and me. Every time Jordan would come over we'd give him so much Indian food. He liked Indian ice cream and Indian cake. Even though Jordan was five years younger than me, I was a bit jealous of him, not in a bad way, but in a good way. I was so proud of him that he knew all the presidents in order. I still don't know them to this day.

Rhonda's Note

We had a wonderful family that lived next door and we adopted each other. Jordan played with the children everyday. Somehow they didn't mind Jordan being different. They treated him like a sibling. They were extremely patient with Jordan, which was wonderful, since it did take him awhile to learn how to interact, share, and learn how to play. After a couple of years of consistency, Jordan did learn how to play.

Ankur, Swati, Manisha, Mili, and Jordan celebrate his birthday.

October 31, 1995

Jordan, for Halloween I dressed you up as a Chicago Bear's football player. You looked so cute. It's raining but Daddy took you out anyway. All the way around the block, you don't really get the concept of Halloween.

Our friend Swati took your hand and guided you through the motions of trick or treat with your bag. Later we took you by our family members so they could see you in costume and you could work on getting that bag full! Grandma Linda is still not speaking to me, so we didn't hear from her or anyone else on my side. Sue sent you a card.

<u>November 1, 1995</u>
Auntie JoJo stopped by with a gift: roller skates! Cool! We went out today and you had fun, with my help of course. A new thing of yours is that you stand in front of the door at 8:30 a.m. and at 3:30 p.m. watching the school buses go by our house. You start yelling out, "Big school bus!" as each one passes. You also do this Curly shuffle dance when you are excited. It looks like Curly's dance from the 3 Stooges. Jordan, you also love the TV show Married with Children.

As soon as the Cheers show is over, you come running from wherever you are and plop yourself on the couch to watch Married with Children. You whip your head around when you hear the theme song; you LOVE it!

<u>December 2, 1995</u>
Today you drew a lovely picture on my hallway wall…at first I reacted and called you a bad boy. Then I corrected myself promptly and said, "No, you are a good boy, Jordan. You just did a bad thing. Your drawing is lovely, only it needs to be on paper, not on my wall." I gave you some paper to draw on and cleaned my wall. Later in the day you emptied an entire roll of toilet paper into the toilet. Oh brother! What a day! Here's a great gain, you were tugging on my leg and ran into the bathroom and whipped off your diaper, and pooped. I was so pleased. Daddy praised you and so did I. You are a big boy. Everyone I know always said you'd go when you were ready.

Rhonda's Note
Around this same period, we visited my friend's mother who had recently bought a new puppy. While all the other kids gath-

ered around the puppy, Jordan flipped through a magazine. He showed no interest in the puppy at all. My friend Mary Jane was speechless when she saw Jordan's reaction, or lack thereof.

Excerpt Friend Mary Jane

I recall Rhonda and Jordan dropping by to see my mother's new puppy. As the visit went on we noticed that Jordan was more interested in the story that was in a magazine than the puppy. My mom said to me that she noticed Jordan didn't seem to interact with my niece Tiffany, nor with the puppy. This was strange. I brought this to Rhonda's attention that it concerned me. So I did some research on my own. I went to the library to check out a book on autism. I was shocked to find out that Jordan's characteristics were similar to those of autism. Knowing what I found, I had to tell Rhonda so she could research this. I am glad that Rhonda took immediate action. Jordan wouldn't be where he is today if it weren't for her quick action to get the help he needed early as a toddler.

Excerpt Friend Cindy

I volunteered to go with Rhonda for her case study meeting. After sitting on the side of the teacher for so long and being the bearer of bad news, I was prepared for Rhonda to break down, but instead she felt empowered.

She was glad to have the help and a game plan for how to support Jordan. With this plan he was able to start preschool.

December 9, 1995

Tomorrow you begin preschool. I received the results of the schools' case study and you were accepted. They said you would need Speech and Social Structure. You have a very nice speech teacher, Miss Jill. Miss Becky and Miss Kathy are also very friendly, and so I am very comfortable with you in their good hands. I will be driving you to and from school until winter break. Then the school bus will pick you up and drop you off. Class will be from 12:30 p.m. to 3:30 p.m. It's kind of scary for me to be entrusting you to other people. I realize there is a God and that it'll be okay.

December 21, 1995

On your first day of preschool I walked you up to the door and the teacher turned you around and walked into the school as you cried your little heart out. The second day was the same routine and the same reaction. By the third day you whimpered and went right in. You seem to like it now. You paint, color, read and play. The teachers really seem to have taken a liking to you. Then again, who wouldn't? You are so cute! Today you brought home a Christmas gift. It was a picture of your little hands with a cute little saying on it. Dad and I cried. It's so neat—our very first gift; we'll treasure it forever. However, you are my greatest gift of all, thank you, Jordan.

Rhonda's Note

After feeling stunned and shocked by Jordan's speech teacher's observation of PDD (pervasive development disorder), it didn't take me very long to come to terms with it. I was faced with a sink or swim situation. Had I chose sink, I would not sink alone. My child would drown. Once I had put my choices into perspective, I knew there was no choice. Rick had moved forward like a steady ship and I needed to get a grip. I realized that early intervention would be the key, and it was definitely vital. I needed to step up to the plate in order to help Jordan.

We wanted him to live a normal life, so we were willing to go to any lengths to help him.

Excerpt Cousin Mike

We were all informed that Jordan was observed as autistic. It was very scary to me. The only autism I was familiar with was from the movie *"Rainman."* Being very naïve and not familiar with autism, the easiest way to deal with this would have been to withdraw. However, this was not an option. We all needed to teach Jordan, at a very young age, that quitting would not be acceptable. So we all buckled down for what we all thought would be a very long ride.

December 30, 1995

The holidays are almost over. You definitely are aware of Santa Claus, but you still don't have the concept. We're trying to establish traditions for you. Saint Nick Day is where you leave candy in your shoes at the front door. I have you leave a letter for Santa to make sure he gets your desires. I also want to teach you to care for others. Like helping out at the homeless organizations in the food kitchens, or the coat drives. Hey! You're starting to talk a little more. You have all the Barney tapes memorized! I still can't understand everything you say. You have been talking to someone named Zoe, maybe he's your spirit guide? I wish you could get a little more grounded on this earth plane.

It seems like you are in and out of here. Back to Christmas, it was so wonderful. You received many nice gifts. Oh, we need to call Auntie JoJo. It's her birthday today.
I love you, Jordan. XOXOXOXO

January 1, 1996: A New Year
Thank God. Phewww.

January 4, 1996
Your newest thing is that you will pretend to sneeze or cough and then say, "Excuse me." Another thing you have been doing is throwing yourself on the ground and saying, "ouch, that hurts," So cute. After school you cried today, this is the first time this has ever happened. Your teacher and I write to each other in a notebook, and she mentioned that you had received a timeout. No wonder you were upset. She said when timeout was over and you obeyed the rules. Good boy, Jordan.

January 8, 1995
Jordan, you are a crazy man today. You have been running through the house like a tornado. You are very active and so strong willed. You will not let me help with anything. All day you have been dancing and singing in front of the mirror. You love to watch yourself.

February 12, 1996
Today is a day off from school, so as a family we drove downtown to the Shedd Aquarium. You wore me out with all this excitement. You ran up and down all the hallways and were mesmerized by each tank we passed. We didn't dare pull you away until you were ready to go for fear of an instant meltdown. You would also gasp, "Look at all the fish!" You really got into the dolphin show. It was very difficult when it was time to leave because you wanted to stay. These situations have become more and more stressful for me. You become very upset and I feel like I don't have control

over you or the situation. You did a bad thing today. You loaded up the slots of my vacuum cleaner with pennies. Oh well, pretty observant to make the connection.

February 18, 1996

Daddy and I were watching a program on "Can you be harboring a Genius, The Next Einstein." Cool. Then they were talking about reincarnation and in fact how these children could be old souls coming to this lifetime with knowledge from past lifetimes. Dad and I were told you're an old soul and I do know there's a lot in that little mind of yours waiting to unfold. Yesterday you counted to 10 in Spanish. That came from your placemat.

February 25, 1996

This was the worst night. You and I went to Justin's birthday party. While we were there, you fell down the stairs. I mean you took a fall and it scared the shit out of me! I was uncomfortable and it didn't get any easier for me. We went to the Discovery Zone where we played in these huge tunnels that went all over the place. You were having a lot of fun there. When it came time to rejoin the party, you resisted and put up a fight. So I continued following you through the tunnels for an hour. When you make up your mind to something, that's it. No one can tell you to do anything different. When we were leaving, you resisted very loudly with your outbursts and you drew a lot of attention. It's very embarrassing and I feel like I have no control over this. I'm also feeling like I'm a failure at times. I cried my eyes out all the way home.

March 24, 1996

You are really testing me and our poor dog, Misty. You keep

pushing her around and she's so old. You have been real sick and we went to see Dr. Carlos.

I have to say she has a good bedside manner with you and has you right where she wants you. Doctors have been hard for you and I get really stressed knowing I have to take you in. Your vocabulary is developing well. You are still repeating everything and you have **huge temper tantrums.**

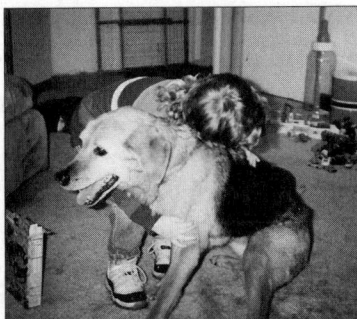

Rhonda's Note
Even though I investigated support groups, I didn't join a local group because the children were the wrong fit and extremely low functioning. I couldn't relate or build relationships and therefore, wouldn't get my much-needed support. Jordan couldn't be compared to anyone I knew out there and I felt so very alone. All the information I received was so generalized on autism, so none of it really answered questions or gave me any direction. This was just another motivating factor for me to continue writing the "Jordan Journal."

<u>April 4, 1996</u>
Jordan, you are killing me. I am so tired all the time. You FIGHT ME TOOTH AND NAIL WITH EVERY-THING. Dressing you is a project in itself. I hope this passes quickly! You are insisting that you pick out your own school clothes. Here's an example of what you'd wear: Striped shirt, totally different color pants and in spring

you'd insist on wearing your winter boots. I Can't fight with you on this, so whatever. I am learning that some things just aren't worth fighting over.

April 13, 1996

Daddy and I took you to the Value City Furniture store. You wouldn't stay with us! When it came time to leave, you had an **enormous tantrum.** You won't let me hold your hand when we cross traffic. You are so strong willed and I can only hope there is reasoning around the corner. Another thing you're doing (that we are trying work with you on) is hugging. You are backing into us rather than facing us when we hug. Daddy and I turn you around and make you hug us facing forward.

May 5, 1996

Our dog Misty turned 20 today. Daddy rented a very large birthday card sign for the front yard. We went out and when we returned there were all kinds of presents for Misty by the front door. People in our neighborhood are very caring. Misty had a great birthday.

May 6, 1996

Your teachers, Miss Becky and Miss Kathy, suggested you should be put in summer school. I agree no time should be lost with hands-on speech and occupational therapy. We also agree that keeping a routine seems to be good for you. Miss Becky came to our house to visit you. My goodness, you were so shy, and it seemed to throw you that she was in our house and out of her element of school.

May 12, 1996

I went to the school today for Mothers' Day Tea. Very cute. They served the mothers tea, cookies and ice cream. Then the classroom all sang a song with hand motions. It was the "Skimmer a Rinky-dink, I love you" song. I did everything not to cry as you motioned to me 'I love you' and of course I melted. Today was a good day for toilet training; two days in a row you pooped. Good job, buddy.

Right now I converse for you. I pray that next year your communication will be improving and you'll be talking to me. I love you soooooooooo much.

June 7, 1996

Oh, you're all over and getting into things. I'm so tired. So much has happened. Aunt Susie (Sue B is what you call her) already has cerebral palsy and now she has been diagnosed with multiple sclerosis and is paralyzed from the waist down. She has been in the hospital for eight weeks, plus she needs rehabilitation. Rough stuff. Susie has had a hard life. I was seven when my mom went door-to-door for volunteers to try this experimental therapy for her rare epilepsy. It gave her brain damage. In my home, growing up was like a circus for eight years. We had over a hundred people a week coming to our house to do therapy with Sue. Fifteen hours everyday, now this, poor Sue.

July 6, 1996

We went to the park today and you climbed into a rocket ship with these little girls. You are so polite. You said, "excuse me, honey." The one girl hits the other girl and says, "Did you hear what he called me? HE CALLED ME HONEY!" What a crackup! You are too cute. You also remind people, like Daddy, to say excuse me when they pass gas. What a parrot you are, repeating everything we say.

July 8, 1996

You start summer school today and will go through August 2nd. Hip, Hip, Hooray! You have the same teacher, Miss Kathy, and the same bus driver, Miss Debbie. This is your first day and you were a bear. You said, "I'm sleepy." (I asked for progress, and you are expressing yourself!)

Your schedule is up at 6:30 a.m. and catching the bus at 8:15 a.m. This is a change for you since you were sleeping in until 10 in the morning. You'll be home at 12:15 p.m. We have your bedtime at 9 p.m. Sometimes you take a nap between two and three. If we see that school goes well, this will be your schedule. We spend a lot of time in our yard so I've been wishing for a fence in the worst way.

I totally freaked because you'll be in the front then in a split second, you're in the backyard.

August 2, 1996

Daddy took you to your second Cubs game. A group of you rented a couple of buses. I'm a nervous wreck. But Daddy seemed totally fine with it. You're on the move so we'll see how you do later on. You're memorizing a lot lately. You know all the planets and almost all the presidents of the United States. Oh, guess what, Jordan? Your puppy was born August 17, 1996. Barkley is her name; she's a chocolate lab. Since we named you after Michael Jordan we wanted your puppy to have a name that would go with that. We named your puppy Barkley after Charles Barkley, another basketball All-Star. Barkley's parents are really cool.

Her dad is named Moses and he's black. Barkley is brown like her mom, Autumn. Barkley will be here for your 4th birthday. You need some company. Misty our dog is too old for you to hug. At 20, she's too fragile. I can't wait until we get Barkley. I'm so excited for you.

Excerpt Cousin Mike

The flashcard training never stopped. In fact it was moved to greater levels. Now Jordan was memorizing each of the president's terms of office, their birthdays and even when they died. Also he would know all of the wrestlers by their entry music. Even though Jordan couldn't communicate vocally, we all knew his favorite wrestlers by his actions. Actions from Jordan were greatly noticed by us because this is how he communicated with us. It made you pay close attention to all the little things. There was huge progress weekly.

August 3, 1996
Daddy wanted me to mention at the Cubs game that everyone on the bus mooned the second bus that was next to yours on the expressway. Daddy pulled your pants down and stuck your bottom up next to the window. I guess you were a hit. It seemed everyone on the second bus got a kick out of it!

August 27, 1996
Your vocabulary is still increasing. However, you still aren't communicating. I went into your school today to meet your teacher Miss Joanne. You still have Miss Becky. She loves you. You have a nice classroom and everything is going great.

Excerpt Preschool & Kindergarten Teacher JoAnn

I first met Jordan when he attended the Early Childhood Program in the Community Consolidated School District #93.

Jordan was a child who appeared to be eager to please and demonstrated many rotary memory skills far above his age level. When presented with letters and numbers he was able to identify them. Another skill that amazed me was his ability to identify the photos of all the past presidents of the United States out of order. While Jordan excelled at skills that involved visual memory, using and understanding words was difficult for him. His limited vocabulary inhibited his ability to interact with his peers and adults. This resulted in his socialization skills lagging far behind those of his peers. With support, however, he was able to develop this skill and at the end of the Early Childhood Program he was integrated with his typical peers since continued support was provided.

September 4, 1996

Now you know not only every president but also 32 states. You say them very fast. Wow! You're still not potty trained.

September 19, 1996

I received a note home from Jordan's speech teacher Miss Jill:

She commented Jordan did Mr. Potato head today and although he got side tracked a couple of times, he followed one-step directions! Miss Jill was amazed when she was reading a new book to you. She read, "quack, quack" and went to open the little flap to show you the duck, but you already said, "duck." The same happened when she read, "moo, moo" and "oink, oink."

She couldn't tell if you saw the book before or if you

were reading along with her. You're going on four years old and they say you're starting to read words. Wild!

I knew you were a smart boy and I guess we'll see how smart you really are. Jordan, you and I read a book with animal sounds. I don't really know if you remembered or if you are starting to read.

October 4, 1996

A few more days and you'll be four. Lollipop the Clown will be entertaining 14 children that play with you. That's at 10 a.m. on Saturday. Afterwards we're going to Sue's to pick up your new chocolate lab puppy, Barkley. Barkley will be seven weeks old when we pick her up. I'm so excited I can hardly wait. I'm bringing my camera and video. For your family party we have our official cake baker, Grandma Codges. The cake will be a Choochoo train, with clown cupcakes inside.

October 5, 1996

Your favorite movie is "*The Wizard of Oz*," the only movie you will watch in its entirety. You absolutely love it. **This was not a good day**. You ran down the street without any pants on. I went chasing after you. Gosh, I was hot! I gave you a swat on the butt and then you ran all the way back home. I talk and talk and talk. There's only so much I can do. I wonder if you are testing your boundaries. I need you to understand this: the swat is for your own safety. God forbid you would have run out into the street.

October 9, 1996

Your party was a hit, and the children loved Lollipop the
Clown and Grandma Codges' cupcakes. All of your friends
and family gave you a lot of learning toys, which you still
absolutely love. What a lucky guy you are.

Rhonda's Note

*No day was typical. A general day in the life of Jordan went
something like this: Up at 6:30 a.m. and off to school, home for
lunch, and some down time. He usually watched his reflection
in the stove door, as he recited the entire school day. He would
be the teacher and stand up. He then would sit back down and
be different students.*

*He didn't talk until he was four. Words were said but there
was really no communication. Then he would run around the
block 12 times a day, probably for stimulation. I had to watch
him like a hawk because he was very fast. Within seconds he
was halfway down the street. This was the part of my life that
was very lonely.* Sometimes Jordan would take 40 minutes to
examine a truck from every angle and it was often in someone
else's driveway! I didn't dare pull him away because he would
have a tantrum. I tried to keep him surrounded by other children in the hope that he would mimic their behavior. Some
days were successful and others were not.*

October 11, 1996

Jordan, you're starting to talk all of a sudden. I'm having a
problem getting you to keep clothes on. You put up a fight
when I'm trying to get you dressed for school. By the time
the bus comes to pick you up, I'm wound up like a top!
Then you refuse any help to get onto the bus. You hold up

your hands and say sternly, "No Mom." Potty training is getting easier; you are about 75% trained.

October 27, 1996

I'm leaving for eight days to visit Aunt Joan in Arizona. This will be the first time I've ever left you alone with Daddy. This will give the both of you a chance to bond and Mom a chance to relax. I'll miss you. See you in eight days. XOXOXO.

Journal kept by daddy while mom went to Arizona

November 8, 1996

We came home from the airport and napped. We then went to McDonald's where we had lunch and played. For dinner we ordered pizza from Chucks and on the way home from Addison we passed the Best Buy and Jordan said, "That's where Tina works." Did homework.

November 9, 1996

We got up and ate breakfast. Nana came over and got you off to school. I got home at 4:30p.m. and my buddies came over to watch wrestling with us.

November 10, 1996

We woke up to storms. I called the babysitter Kristina to cancel but she had left already. Oh well, I went to work anyway. After I got home, we loaded up my truck with aluminum cans and went to Wal-Mart, Target, and Big K. looking for collector wrestling cars. We spent two hours at Chuck E. Cheese, and went to bed at 8:30 p.m.

<u>November 11, 1996</u>

We went to IHOP for breakfast. Then we drove downtown to the recycling place. When I turned down Western Avenue Jordan said, "This is where we go see Nitro wrestling, Dad." I drove through the Lower Wacker, Outer drive, down Michigan Avenue, then onto all the skyscrapers. We saw the United Center, Soldiers' Field, the Museums, Navy Pier and Wrigley Field. Jordan got to stay up for Nitro, we did homework, showered, and then to bed.

<u>November 12, 1996</u>

I had a hard time getting Jordan up after two days off. Nana came over and took you shopping. She said you had a blast.

<u>November 13, 1996</u>

Annamea bailed me out. I couldn't find a sitter. Carla and Laura had plans. We ate at a Greek place then we went bowling. Jordan started asking everyone for a dollar, so I put a stop to that. I must have spent $25 on games alone. On the way home from bowling Jordan asked to stop for sliders at White Castle; yep, he's mine. As much junk as he ate, he fell right asleep once we got home.

<u>November 14, 1996</u>

We went bowling, then out shopping. Jordan found some magnets with names on them. He drew a crowd as he proceeded to read them all.

<u>November 15, 1996</u>

We went to the airport to get you, Mom. I have no clue how single people raise children. It's amazing how much attention they need. Jordan missed you, and I missed you too. As we were waiting for you to come off the plane Jordan had every-one around involved in counting and waiting for you to get off the plane. When you finally got off everyone was cheering. Too, too cute. This kid knows how to draw a crowd.

November 18, 1996
You decided it was time to wear big boy underwear. All that effort it took trying to get you to go on the potty and BAM!!! At school you wanted nothing to do with Pull-ups. It is underwear or nothing else will do. Two days have passed and you pooped on the toilet, simply amazing.

November 19, 1996
Well, Dad and I took you to your very first movie. Space Jam. I was a mess freaking out the entire time and Dad acted like it was no big thing. You were talking and getting up and down from your seat. You kept hitting the little boy's chair in front of you. Dad needs to take you more often. Nothing bothers him. After work we took you to Chuck E. Cheese and played a little. Oops, you went potty in your underwear and we had to leave because I didn't bring a change of clothes.

November 20, 1996
On this morning I was giving you a choice between black and white gym shoes. You would say "No, Mommy, boots." Finally I raised my voice and said "Jordan, why do you do this to me?" and your response was, "Why not?"

November 21, 1996
Your favorite movie is The Lion King. You watch it over and over and over. Today you tried to feed the goldfish and dumped the whole can of food in the bowl-ahhhhgg!

November 25, 1996

It's Thanksgiving and we went to Auntie JoJo's and Uncle Dave's. I enjoyed myself, but Dad was sick. He laid around and watched TV. You on the other hand ran up and down the stairs playing with all the children. This was a nice change of pace. Auntie Jo bought you a nice car set. She picks out neat gifts.

November 29, 1996

Misty our dog passed away. We are very sad and you keep calling for her. You open the door and whistle. I told you she went to heaven and you said, "No heaven, Mommy." You're starting to string words together. Very cool.

December 7, 1996

Our neighbor Carla's father dressed as the German traditional St. Nick. He gave you a bag of candy and an apple. You were shy, but took the gift. Sunday you went on your first train ride to the North Pole to pick up Santa. This was through the park district. At the Hanover Park Train Station they served hot cocoa and cookies and off we went to pick up the fat man in the red suit. For the ride a woman read the story *The Polar Bear Express*. At our destination we met Santa and he rode back to Hanover Park with us. That was pretty neat.

December 24, 1996

Christmas morning you slept in late. We helped you open gifts from Santa. Hey, you got a bus, Cookie Monster, learning toys, and other nice gifts. You understand now the meaning of who Santa is. We went over to Grandma Linda's and my Father was there. This was the first family dinner in over 15 years, and it's pretty weird. Divorce creates strange feelings. You have been talking up a storm still and it keeps getting better.

January 4, 1997

On New Year's Eve, you stayed up until 12:00 a.m. We went to Chuck E. Cheese with my friend Pat and her daughter Jenna. I'm proud of you. When it was time to go you left quietly. No tantrums. We also went shopping at Target where you even helped me push the shopping cart.

January 28, 1997

Jordan, you are enjoying your dog Barkley so much. You play tug-of-war with her. You put her toys in your mouth and Barkley takes the other end. You each pull hard, and I think this is so great that you're so close. Barkley also bites you and you bite her back, she chases you and you chase her. It's as though you become a puppy too. It's really cute when she puts her paw on your shoulder—best buddies: Barkley and Jordan.

February 8, 1997

Today was a long, long day. We took you to see "*Toy Story*" on Ice, you were mesmerized. You were so intense that you almost peed right in your seat. I looked and you had your pants down and were ready to go! I caught you just in time.

February 23, 1997

You are now talking really great in complete sentences. I also have been working with flash cards to help you remember the presidents of the United States, the planets, shapes and colors. Sometimes you forget a few of the presidents, but in two days of review you have them mastered. Crafts are your newest activity. Gluing, painting, and cutting with scissors. You're still having trouble sleeping in your own bed. You want to sleep with Mommy and Daddy. We even purchased a really cool loft bed thinking you would love it and want to sleep in it. It is not happening though.

March 10, 1997

Jordan you still mimic everything. I bought you a "Say No to Drugs" tape and you mimic everything including the beginning where a handicapped girl sings all choppy. (You copy her by also singing choppy). You're getting better at communicating and it makes life a little more fun for me, too.

March 20, 1997

This week we took you for a hearing test, I wasn't sure if you could hear me. There are times when you don't respond. The woman held the earphones to your ears, every time you heard a beep you put a piece of puzzle together. To our surprise you followed directions perfectly. You also recently took an interest in the game of soccer. Ben, our neighbor, plays in his front yard and you always want to go out to play when you see him. The Easter bunny is going to bring you a soccer ball and a net.

March 21, 1997

You got *"Space Jam,"* the Michael Jordan video and you watch it everyday! During the one scene when Bugs Bunny kisses Michael Jordan, you go running

through the house to find one of us and you give us a big old kiss. It's so cute. You also make a muscle like Bugs Bunny in the video. You seem to watch the same video over and over until you've memorized it and then you start another.

<u>Easter 1997</u>

You are pretty cool, Jordan. We took you on an Easter egg hunt and you loved it! The bunny was there and you had ice cream, colored Easter eggs and all your neighborhood friends came: Mili, Ankur, Swati, Manisha, your cousin Krystal, Jered and Justin…Wow!

The Easter Bunny was good to you, too. He left a huge basket of all kinds of neat things. Bubbles, soccer ball, a bat and ball—man, are you lucky. I didn't get to videotape you; regretfully, my camera is broken. Xoxoxox Mom.

April 1997 (Jordan, four years old)

I went to observe you at school. I was talking to your teachers, Miss Jill and Miss Becky and they believe you have Autistic tendencies. When you run you look back and watch your feet. You have an outstanding memory, so with all that I'm going to take you to see Doctor Swisser at Children's Memorial Hospital. I hear he is an excellent Neurologist.

<u>April 1997</u>

Jordan, you came up to me today and asked me to write my name. I said, "Tell me how to spell it," and you spelled Mom. You then asked me to spell Dad. I asked you to spell it and you spelled Rick! You can also spell Barkley and Sneakers our cat. I found out that Walt Disney and Einstein had Autistic tendencies. Today I walked into the bathroom and you had the toilet lid off. I asked what you were doing and your response was "where does the poop go?" HAHAHAHA

May 8, 1997

I started you on a vitamin program; I noticed a big difference with your communication. You have a big boy bike
now. Ankur gave you his and my goodness are you proud!
Yesterday our neighbor Carla was walking down the street
and noticed you walking your bike. She said, "Jordan is that
your new bike?" Proud as a peacock you mounted the bike
and started to ride.

Excerpt Friend Chickie

I noticed Jordan displayed repetitive behavior, such as turning
around and looking at his heels as he walked. Another thing he
did was to walk back and forth the length of the mirrors on the
closets. Rhonda spoke to me about experimenting with Jordan's
diet and adding vitamins. She continued spending many hours
teaching him and keeping him focused.   The results were
astounding. When I visited him four weeks later, I saw a dra-
matic change in Jordan. He actually saw me. He acknowledged
me without being told to. It was the first time I saw him smile.
He didn't communicate with one or two words anymore. He
was now putting together sentences and using words I never
heard him use before. He showed other emotions besides the
tantrums he threw when he couldn't do what he pleased. The
repetitive behavior was still there, but not as pronounced.

May 27, 1997

Today I attended a meeting at school and your progress is
exceptional. I have all my ducks in a row for the tests at

Children's Memorial Hospital. I'm videotaping clips of you doing certain things that might be considered a little different or in some cases exceptional. I wonder what the doctor will think.

I would like it, if in the hour we spend with him, he feels as if he knows you.

Rhonda's Note

For a further, professional diagnosis, we took Jordan to Children's Memorial Hospital in Chicago, Illinois. (I received a referral from a friend I met in a sign language class. At one point I didn't know if Jordan was going to talk at all, so I attended a class to learn how to sign.) I would recommend this to any parent whose child is experiencing delayed communication.

We saw a wonderful Doctor. Dr. Charles Swisser. We were hoping for the most accurate diagnosis possible. Considering Dr. Swisser never met Jordan prior to his appointment and the doctor would only see him for one hour, I put together a montage of our videotapes that showed Jordan's idiosyncrasies. I requested the doctor view it right away. He did and was very impressed with my method, saying it was the best idea from a parent in all his experience and asked to keep my tape.

Dr. Swisser indicated that if he could go out on a limb, he would venture to say that Jordan, in or around third grade, would lose most of the outward signs of autism. He did explain that Jordan had Pervasive Developmental Disorder which falls under the umbrella of autism.

Dr. Swisser also suggested that I surround him with children. He explained that Jordan was a visual learner and his final comment to me was "Keep the Kool-aid pitcher filled!" This was very important advice...I kept that Kool-aid pitcher filled and I thanked God for having the great neighbors that we had.

May 28, 1997

Dr. Charles Swisser. He believes you have a mild case of P.D.D. so, in other words, a mild case of autism. He also seems to feel this label might not even apply by the time you start grade school. You are what is called a visual learner. You follow what other people do. This is why Daddy and I have been surrounding you with other children. I guess it was instinct that made us do it.

June 5, 1997

I walked downstairs today and you were writing. I asked you what you were doing. You answered, "Writing Mom." I walked over to see, and that's what you were doing...writing! I am keeping your first written words. You wrote, "I love you Mom-Der Jordan to Jordan."

Excerpt Godmother JoJo (Directed to Jordan)

When I was told about your autism I remember feeling a calm come over me. I knew with all my soul that everything was going to be okay. The wonderful thing that sticks out in my heart was how your parents refused to treat you any different. They were determined to help you every step of the way.

June 20, 1997

I decided to give you a shorter haircut. I can't get myself to cut the back short! Sometimes your scalp is really sensitive to the comb and brush so I have to cut your hair when you're sleeping. Today we went to a birthday party for one of your classmates at McDonald's. Seeing your classmates outside of school was exciting for you and we all had lots of fun. Now that school is out you want to be outside from 12 p.m. to 8 p.m. I can barely get you inside to eat lunch and dinner. Today I'm taking Swati, Ankur, Mili, and their cousins to Chuck E. Cheese and to the Rainbow Park. My plan is to take you somewhere every week. Your newest thing is going up to every mailbox on the block and opening them. This is on the way to the park everyday. We always have to take a certain way home, so in some cases it could take 45 minutes to walk to the park at the end of the block. Your speech is getting clearer and clearer. You ask some questions now and then. You write short notes to me. What is amazing is I never taught you how to write or spell. Xoxooxo Mom.

Excerpt Friend Jane

I have heard that people who are Autistic sometimes have amazing abilities in other mental areas such as musical abilities beyond belief, or mathematical abilities far superior to those of a normal person. It turned out that Jordan had some remarkable abilities with memory. Jordan used this placemat his mom had gotten him with the presidents of the United States. He developed a game. I could give him a president's name and he would tell me where that president was in the order of all the presidents. For example: Abraham Lincoln would elicit an answer of 16. Or I would give him a number and he would tell me which president it was. I could only tell you that I don't know any adults including myself that can do that. It was a good thing I had the placemat when we played the presidents game, or I wouldn't have had a clue about any of them except the most obvious. I should mention this was long before kindergarten. I call Jordan "Mr. President."

July 30, 1997

Words you can spell: elephant, stop, go, cat, dog, fish, green and much more. Talking is coming along as well. You seem to enjoy basketball and baseball. You stay focused when we watch or try to play these games. Also you are a very fast runner. You are a whiner lately, and it cuts my skin like a knife, I can't stand it. Jordan, you are funny. You moon Daddy and make all sorts of funny faces. Most of all, the children in the neighborhood love to play with you. Daddy and I have been taking you to all the festivals in the surrounding area and you just love the rides. At the DuPage County Fair your Daddy took you on the tilt a whirl and he turned GREEN! He got out of the ride running into the field and got sick. Hahahaha! :)

August 17, 1997

Barkley's first birthday. Something so cute happened today. Swati was lying on the ground. You then laid on top of her and while the two of you were linked you both rolled down the grass together. The both of you were laughing so hard; it was great. Swati is really good with you. I secretly hope you find a girl like her one day. She is so wonderful. You are into Winnie the Pooh and the book Spot the Dog. You are also going around knocking on our neighbors' doors and telling the women (moms) that they are gorgeous. You are also kissing and hugging all the girls. You are quite the little flirt at five.

<u>**August 27, 1997**</u>

When Mommy and Daddy come home now, you get so excited and start running all around and yelling "Mommy's home, Mommy's home!" Lately when I'm out driving, if I don't go the way you want me to go, you'll start having tantrums. Today I did not turn right at County Farm road. We arrived home with you crying non-stop. I went into the house and you stayed in the truck. After watching you for what seemed like a long time, I knew you wouldn't stop until I drove back to the corner of Army Trail Road and County Farm Road and made that right turn, so I did. You stopped crying. I can't get over how intense your screaming is. It is like scratching nails on a blackboard. I often feel like I myself want to scream along with you.

<u>**August 29, 1997**</u>

You were playing Pac-Man and you mimicked Dad cussing and said, "Dommik!" We both started laughing because it sounded funny. We then taught you that "Oh shucks" is better to say.

<u>**August 31, 1997**</u>

It's been a long day. We went to Uncle Eddies' birthday party. It was nice because you played with Krystal. Today I am in a very sad place. Princess Diana of England died in a car crash. I only have been saddened by one other celebrity death. John Lennon. Elvis Presley's death didn't make me cry. Princess Diana's death seems so senseless. I feel sad for her two boys William and Harry who will miss her. Mother Theresa is another icon of our times. She did a lot for the poverty stricken people of Calcutta. Both of these women were beautiful and gracious. We had two deaths and the news of a birth today. Carla had a baby today, how exciting. We also had to attend a wake for Dad's Uncle Jerry. You were really loud, but cute. This world keeps on going with or without us, Jordan.

September 9, 1997
You called the police today!! You hit the button on the phone and they were knocking on my door. "Is everything okay in here?" I said, "I didn't call, it must have been Jordan!" You stinker. Some other things you are saying: "Basket, basket, whoa, whoa, whoa. Orange, orange, whoa, whoa, whoa. Coffee, Coffee, whoa, whoa, whoa." It must be from a song? You call Edie "Codges" and Swati says it sounds like the Indian word for eyeliner.

October 6, 1997 (Jordan's fifth birthday)
With every gift that you opened carefully, you gave a comment and a thank you. "Oh, a very cute Winnie the Pooh shirt, thank you." "Oh, very nice pants for school, thank you." You are so cute.

October 22, 1997
I went shopping for a Christmas gift for you from Nana. I picked you out a lot of crafty things. You love to play school. Auntie Jo thinks you may be a professor when you grow up. Who knows she may be right.

October 25, 1997
Dad is writing in your journal:

Jordan, Mom is gone for a few days and it's just you and me. Today in Pac-Man you've made it to the first key and that's hard to do! You're my little genius. Mom is on vacation, and Jordan and I stopped at the McDonald's on Mannheim to quiet Jordan down (Jordan had a meltdown). We had a wonderful time on Monday. We went to three parks and drove to Lombard's Haunted House. Mike got you ready for school on Tuesday and we ordered pizza for dinner and stayed home. Wednesday, Mike helped out again by getting you off to school. For dinner you and I went out to Chuck E. Cheese and we got pumpkins too. Thursday I had some problems getting you dressed for school. I helped out at school and we saw a parade. We stopped to show Nana and Papa your costume. We picked up Nikita and took all the kids trick or treating. We came home, warmed up and went back out again, fun time. All week we spent time together, I took you with me for bowling and even to play poker. We also went and did a few job estimates. We ate out quite a bit, and guess what? White Castles…You love them!!!! I've told you that tomorrow we pick up mom. I don't know how single parents do this day in and out! Children need so much attention. Love, Dad.

October 26, 1997
Today we took a ride to Brookfield Zoo. Swati, Mili, Ankur, Grandma, and Aunt Sue went also. We all had a great time trick or treating.

October 31, 1997
Halloween was fun and you were Bugs Bunny. I brought the whole gang of kids with us. You ran up to the houses and opened the doors yelling, "Trick or Treat!" You didn't understand the knocking on the door part. We filled your pump-

kin twice. Dad and I were room parents for you and we loved it. We played games like pass the pumpkin and Bozo's Buckets. I made sure there were tons of cool prizes like bubbles and spider rings.

Swati, Mili, Manisha, and Jordan

November 21, 1997

This is cute. While I was getting dressed you asked me, "Where is your penis, Mommy?" I explained that girls have vaginas and boys have penises. You walked into the next room and told Dad that Barkley had a vagina. Dad almost fell off the couch! He asked me, "What did he say?" We laughed when I explained the conversation you and I had. You are naturally curious, and I love that about you.

November 23, 1997

You are so sweet when I'm watching TV. If I cry, you get upset and comfort me. You say, "Don't cry mom." And then you hug and kiss me. You will also brush my hair away from my forehead and bring me a tissue.

Thanksgiving 1997

We spent this holiday at Nana and Papa's house. You really understand what is going on this year. You insisted on having dinner with the adults.

December 5, 1997

We were watching Channel 11. There was an Italian opera star singing. You went up to the TV and began to mimic her facial and hand expressions. It was hilarious. I encouraged you to keep going. You were also·singing along with her.

December 6, 1997

We took you to see Christmas lights at Candy Cane Lane. You were so excited that you kept screaming, "Look Mom, Look Mom, Look Mom." You say it over and over. You've been testing me a lot lately and at times I feel like I am at a breaking point.

December 24 & 25 1997

Christmas Eve Dad had to work. Being a landscaper has its disadvantages. I was up all night helping Santa display your toys. Santa got you a nice big calendar for your walls, just like school. There's a weather center and a helper caterpillar. I punched all this out by hand so I didn't get to sleep till 2:45 a.m. When you woke up, you were thrilled and played school all morning. Later we went to Grandma Linda's to open gifts. It was a pleasant and peaceful day.

December 26, 1997

Christmas was a lot of fun this year because you now understand it. We spent time with Dad's family and tomorrow we will go with Codges to downtown Chicago. We will have lunch at Marshall Fields in the Walnut room. Dad had played Santa for your classroom. There's a boy with Down Syndrome in your class. He sat on Dad's lap and hugged him so tight and then he gave Dad a big kiss.

The teachers told us that he's never done this before and it was a break through for him. This made Dad cry. You, however, knew it was Dad and you were a bit jealous.

December 27, 1997

I took you riding around looking at Christmas decorations. You yell out, "Slowly, slowly, look, look, beautiful Christmas." Hey, you're even singing Jingle Bells now!

January 27, 1998

Oh man are you testing us lately. If I tell you "no," then you go to Dad. It's been starting trouble between Dad and me. During the summer you only answer to me, so when Dad is home in the winter it messes up our routine. I raised my voice at you today. You grabbed my cheeks and said in a scolding voice "Stop that Mommy, don't do that." You are a handful. Lately you've become a wizard at Nintendo. I can't wait to see you on the computer.

February 8, 1998

This evening we went out to dinner. You wouldn't sit with us. You insisted on your own table. Dad picked you up to sit you at our table and you screamed soooooo loud! Dad had to pick you up and carry you out with everyone looking. You carried on for 45 minutes.

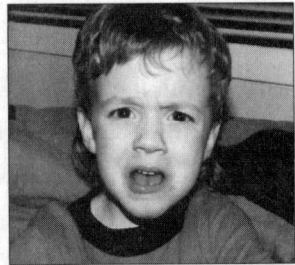

February 18, 1998

This morning you were talking in your sleep. I asked you

about it and you said that you were wrestling Scott Hall. You are very much into World Class Wrestling. You love Hulk Hogan, Rick Flair, and Macho Man. You are nonstop leg dropping, elbow smashing, head butting and drop kicking and after school you wrestle yourself everyday on Mom's bed. I think it's giving you some sort of stimulation.

March 31, 1998
A whole bunch of us went to Monday night Nitro wrestling. Our friend John was dressed up as Sting. It was hilarious; you thought the real Sting was sitting with us! We all had a great time. School is going really well too. You are adding, subtracting, and spelling at the age of five. Understanding directions can be difficult for you. You get this little sad cry face. At Joaquin's birthday party they played games. I could tell you didn't understand the directions to the game. However, most of the time, once you actually saw the game, you could play.

April 21, 1998
Your speech is getting better. I spoke with your speech teacher today. Miss Jill believes the only real problem you might have is your language. You are gifted in many ways and you will need to be challenged in some areas. Introducing new concepts may be hard. Jordan, you are so into wrestling that on Sunday you and Dad bond while you both watch it. Dad shares all his information with you and you take in every bit. I bought you a first grade Reader Rabbit computer game. You've mastered it in no time flat. Amazing!

May 12, 1998
Your new thing is blowing kisses. When Miss Terry the bus driver picks you up she'll say, "Jordan, say good bye to

your Mom." You repeat, "Good bye Mom, Good bye Mom." It's so cute. Also, when I leave to go shopping you'll follow me halfway down the street blowing kisses at me. You'll run and try to keep up with my truck. Dad and I took you to a carnival. You have no fear. You wanted to go on every ride alone. Jordan, you are always shocking me.

June 22, 1998
Your first visit to the dentist and you would not let them touch or come anywhere near you. You were cowering in the corner. Your dentist asked you to open your mouth, but you only let her look in from a distance. Perhaps we'll try again later.

July 12, 1998
You are having an action packed summer. I put you in tap dancing. We are going to mega carnivals, which you love. I stopped a big ride you were on once because I thought you were going to be sick. You couldn't believe I did that. Also, you are in summer school. Keeping structure is so vital. Yesterday we couldn't find you in the house. You were next door with Manisha cuddling on the couch watching TV; so cute.

July 15, 1998
Today you were talking to your make-believe friends, Stash, Gutton, Adam, Mandy, Tim and Zoe. At least I think they might be make believe. You stand in front of my mirror in the salon and make believe you are wrestling your friends. You have "Battle Royals"- two against three. You "beat" yourself up and it's entertaining.

July 22, 1998

Connor's birthday party was today. Peewee golf. I struggled with trying to teach you the game, but you insisted on playing your own way. You wouldn't take instructions from Laura either. Holding the club incorrectly you would hit the golf ball, pick it up and place it into the hole. After a while, you started to get the idea. Sometimes I could pull my own hair out in frustration.

July 28, 1998

Jordan, you're doing really well in tap class. But you hate going there. There were supposed to be two other boys in your class, so now you don't want to go because there are all girls. The reason why I did this was because it is visual learning and this will help you. Summer school is still going beautifully and you are spending a lot of time with Manisha and Swati at their houses.

July 29, 1998

Today we kept you out of school and drove down to Ashland Avenue to meet the wrestler Goldberg. We waited in line three and a half hours. You were really good! When we finally reached the front of the line I asked Goldberg if he would shake your hand. He stood up and said, "It would be my pleasure." What a great guy! Goldberg signed an autograph and we were off. After that we drove down to Navy Pier and took you to the Children's Museum. You couldn't get enough of it. You pretended to be driving a school bus, played with puppets and climbed trees. Then we ate lunch and headed off to your cousins' birthday party. What a fun-packed day!

August 1, 1998

Uncle Eddie totally blew my mind today. He gave you one of his signed and authentic racecars. I cried all the way home. Uncle Eddie was showing his love the only way he knew how. That memory will always be etched in my mind. When I was growing up, we would spend time with family. My grandmother would take me for a week and sometimes two. That's what grandparents did back then. I feel that family members are too busy now. Maybe one of the reasons they may not spend a lot of time with you is because you're so active and a lot of work. Still, how could anyone not want to spoil you rotten? It hurts your Dad and me that you may be missing out on a connection that was so special in our lives.

August 11, 1998

Time is flying and you are still so cute. This is the latest. When you go to bed you say your prayers. After asking God to bless everyone, you end your prayers with "And God bless peanut butter and jelly sandwiches." Who knows where you get this, you are too funny! You really love bowling. You seem to strategically position the ball off the bumpers to strike and spare. Our neighbor Laura was giggling while you were bowling. She said, "Jordan must calculate it all out before he even throws the ball. Who knows what's going on in that brain of his."

6

Trying to Find His Niche

August 26, 1998
I think you had a good time at school today. You came home and acted it all out. Last Monday we took you to WCW Wrestling matches. You were throwing yourself all over the corridor pretending that you were wrestling someone. You were having a ball. I can see it in your eyes when you watch the matches, how much you love it.

September 12, 1998
You started your Bumper Bowling League today. You are on a team with Joel, Charlie, and Mike. In the first frame you got a strike. Your teammates got spares. You guys put your hands on top of each other and threw them into the air yelling "Ya!" I had to be the loudest person yelling in the place!

October 6, 1998 (Jordan's Sixth Birthday)

It's your Golden Birthday, and your class threw you a party. They all drew a picture and made you a really nice card. I made cupcakes and brought juice. Everyone seemed to have a good time. Your birthday party will be on the 11th.

October 11, 1998

All your friends came to celebrate your birthday. There were more than 10 kids all together. I took all of you bowling. Go figure. We were there for almost two hours. You smashed your finger in the ball return and cried your little heart out. You had a great time bowling after you got over it. You managed to get a couple of strikes and spares. The bowling alley made all individual pizzas for everyone. Grandma Codges (remember our cake expert), made very cool bowling ball cupcakes. Later on all of our family members came over for the evening. You received a lot of really neat gifts. There were a lot of learning toys. I push those when asked for suggestions and quite frankly you enjoy them. The Monday after your birthday you went to see Nitro Wrestling (Goldberg, your favorite, was there). You were so tired I let you stay home from school to enjoy a day of well-deserved rest.

October 31, 1998

Your kindergarten class is so cute. I took a lot of pictures; however, I lost the camera. I think I left it at Auntie JoJo's. Your favorite wrestler is Scott Hall. For Halloween, I dressed you to look like him. You copy Scott Hall's motions. You'll move your hands over your head and then point both hands to your side. As you were waiting to be in the school parade, you made that motion to me! Sweet! For bowling everyone dressed up and you went as Goldberg the wrestler. You had to decorate a pumpkin and it was judged. Daddy and I are so lucky, we got to chaperone your kindergarten class to Sunny Acres pumpkin farm.

You don't often express yourself, however my eyes can read you and I know you were enjoying yourself. You are still testing me more and more. You're still very strong willed—you want to teach me and I NEED to teach you! Homework is HARD! I need to explain the directions and ask you questions. This is a constant struggle because you want to do things a certain way...your way. You are still sleeping with Mom and Dad. You will not sleep in your own bed. I've learned some things aren't worth a fight.

November 27, 1998

I went away on vacation. God knows I needed it. I came home to a big boy. You made some progress while I've been gone. You went to Wal-Mart and Burger King with Nana. This is HUGE PROGRESS. You normally would not get into anyone's car but ours (and you wouldn't go with anyone else anywhere). Today to my shock, you went with Myron and Jessie to her bowling party. HIP, HIP, HURRAY! I was told you had a blast and that's great news!

December 24, 1998

Uncle Eddie called you up acting as Santa. The recorder picked up and he was leaving a message, "This is Santa from the North Pole calling for Jordan, HoHoHo." You were screaming for Dad to "Pick-up the phone because it was Santa." We put him on speakerphone so you could tell him a list of everything you wanted. Nintendo 64, Arthur books and some wrestling figures. At one point he asked you to hold on while he asked Rudolph to go get him a beer! We laughed and laughed. You haven't stopped repeating it ever since. I made sugar cookies and your buddies (Swati, Manisha, Mili and Ankur) helped decorate them. Then we watched the Charlie Brown Christmas special. We drove down to Candy Cane Lane, and looked at the lights. You love when we do this and you get very excited.

January 6, 1999
When I was talking to you the other day you told me I was annoying you and I was driving you crazy! That's what I say to you! I love you, my sweet child.

February 16, 1999
We were snuggling and getting ready for bed when you said, "Mommy, today is Aunt Karrie's birthday." I had nothing posted and quite honestly I didn't remember her birthday myself. I called Karrie and I'll be a son of a gun, you were right.

February 29, 1999
Miss Murphy has a program in the classroom where children from the 5th grade come into the classroom and help by reading books to the younger children. Your helper told Miss Murphy that you read the entire book to yourself and obviously didn't need his help. Jordan, you have a remarkable ability to memorize words. At this time, though, we still don't think you comprehend all of the language.

April 5, 1999
You went to Joaquin's birthday party today and there was a puppet show. Most of the children had puppets named Roger Rabbit or other cartoon character names. But oh no,

not my son. When we asked you what your puppet was named, you said, "Lewinsky," as in Monica! Apparently you had been watching the presidential scandal on CNN television. You made everyone laugh.

April 27, 1999

You are noticing bodies, especially women's bodies, particularly breasts. You came home today and announced that your teacher had giant boobs. At least you're noticing things. That's good!

April 28, 1999

I went to your IEP (Independent Evaluation Program) today and received wonderful news. You are making terrific progress. Next year your teacher will be Miss Patti. I heard from Carla that Miss Patti is devoted to her students, heart and soul. You are being divinely guided, my son.

April 29, 1999

Well Jordan, I'm off to London. I'm taking a holiday with Grandma Codges. I'm already missing you. I've never had to experience missing you with this distance between us. An entire ocean and another country! Daddy has a lot planned and I will think of you everyday and probably every minute.

April 30, 1999
Daddy's Journal:

You got to go bowling with the big guys and you wanted to stop on the way home for jalapeno sliders (White Castle burgers). You started crying when we got home because Mom wasn't home. We hugged and I assured you she would be home next Saturday.

May 1, 1999
We got up early to go down to the Cubs game. You are really excited about going. We took a bus and you were the helper, passing out sandwiches and pop. That evening we played basketball in the driveway. You were pooped!

May 2, 1999
This was another early morning. We had to pick up Mike and Spencer for a softball game. There was a park there and you were a mess. It looked like you rolled in mud all day. I gave you a bath and you were asleep by nine.

May 5, 1999
Mike was here at 6:30 a.m. to see you off to school. I had called the school to let them know they were not to put you on the bus. It was raining all day.

I was a little late and you came out of the office crying your little heart out. You were scared. I told you I was sorry and that I didn't mean to make you cry. I took you on a few estimates for work and we came home and watched the lightning and listened to it thunder.

May 6, 1999
Nana picked you up today. She took you to McDonald's to eat and to Blockbuster to rent a game. When I got to the shop you and Papa were playing catch in the backyard. I wish he would have had time to play with me when I was little.

We got home and there was a voice message from

Mommy. You were so excited. We read a book and went to sleep.

May 7, 1999

Boy, oh boy, I don't know what I would have done without Mike. You made a friend at his house. Her name is Olivia. She wants you to come back and play Saturday. We took a nap so you could bowl tonight. God, Jordan, where do you get all that energy?

Love, Daddy

May 8, 1999

This is Mommy. When I came home from London you were at Mike's.

I called you when I arrived and you were so excited. "I love you Mama, you're home, you're home. I love you Mama." You made me start to cry.

You and Daddy came to the airport. When you saw me you ran and jumped, wrapping your legs around my waist so tight and saying over and over, "Mommy, I love you, I missed you, Mama, I'm so glad you're home, Mommy!" Gosh, Jordan, you are the most wonderful gift a person could have. I love you.

Excerpt Friend Diane

I met Rhonda and Jordan through my son's bus driver. My son Joshua is also Autistic. Rhonda has definitely come into our life for a reason. When I met Rhonda, I had just gotten Joshua into the Early Childhood Intervention Class at school. Rhonda has already run the gamut; her dedication, tenacity, love and strength regarding her son was something I greatly admired.

She taught me that my son was a gift and helped me stop think-ing "Why me?" or "Why Joshua?"

June 14, 1999
We went to the zoo today. A lot of fun! Grandma Linda and Aunt Sue came along. You seem really interested in animals all of a sudden. Your favorite today is the giraffe. You look at this particular animal in amazement.

June 16, 1999
Today is your first swim lesson. I'm a little nervous, but besides trembling under the pool's ice cold shower, you seem to be fine. The teacher's name is Steve, and he did a super job with you.

June 17, 1999
Miss Murphy agreed to tutor you for the summer and the progress is apparent. Yeah!

July 13, 1999
Back to swim lessons. Steve is wonderful. You really respond nicely to him. Amber has worked with you a cou-ple of times. You seem to almost tease her. It's very sweet. You are in summer school now. You really want to stay home, but the routine is good for you. We went to the bowling alley today. Great job! You bowled a 155 and 115. I took you to Toys R Us to pick out a WCW wrestling video. You also wandered away from me and I heard your cries. You were saying, "Mama, come back!" My God, Jordan, you almost broke my heart. I would never leave you, honey. I gave you lots of hugs and kisses. We got home and I found

you on the computer looking at LJN wrestling figures on EBay. Now how did you know how to do that? I guess watching Dad on the computer has really paid off for you.

July 20, 1999

We went to a softball tournament and there was this pretty little girl sitting by you. You started flexing your biceps and telling the girl to look at your muscles. You're a funny boy. Jordan, I have to really watch you.

July 21, 1999

At swim lessons today you swallowed a lot of water and up chucked in the pool. That was it for your lesson, you wanted to go home.

Jordan and his cousin Krystal

7

Look at You Now—
Regular Classes!

<u>August 27, 1999 (Jordan, six years old)</u>
I registered you for the First Grade. It's official. It's been a very long summer and two weeks seems so long to wait. I feel we have had an eventful summer, bowling together on a Mother/Son league. We also went to the movie theatre to see Star Wars and Tarzan. I took you shopping almost every week. You had sleepovers, birthday parties, and you've been tutored in summer school. Everyday you played with your friends. I'm also very proud to say that you no longer require Special Education classes. It seems you need to have role models to learn from. Miss Murphy noticed you no longer learn from some of these children. You've moved beyond a lot of them. Praise God. You learn with visual aids and it appears these children can't provide this for you anymore. You miss Swati a lot lately. She's so darn cute. Everyday you ask me when she'll be home from school, and

everyday I tell you the same time. You have this habit of crinkling your nose up at me and you're still mimicking everything I say. You have a few make-believe friends. The same ones you've had for awhile: Stash, Gutton, and Adam. You still have conversations with them all the time. I often hear you try to work through daily events talking things out with them. You sometimes repeat conversations after a friend leaves and you're talking about everything that's been said and replaying it to yourself. Very strange. I don't quite understand this.

<u>**August 30, 1999**</u>

We took a cake to "Uncle Fester" for his birthday. It made him smile. He got that name from you saying over and over Uncle Eddie 15 times straight. He turned to you and said, "My name isn't Uncle Eddie, it's Uncle Fester." Without skipping a beat you said Uncle Fester five more times and it stuck. You get a lot of headaches, but what's funny is that whenever Connor comes over to play Nintendo with you, you'll come running to me saying, "Mommy, it's a miracle! My headache is gone."

<u>**September 5, 1999**</u>

First Grade. You should understand that you are divinely guided. You have been blessed with a teacher who is truly an Angel. Miss Patti is her name and I hit it off with her right away. She seems to understand your needs. Elsie Johnson School is fabulous. Everyone is working as a team to help you meet all of your goals. You need a full-time aide and there are no "ifs," "ands," or "buts," about it! All of your lessons need to be broken down first to help you understand them. Concepts are difficult for you to understand at first, but again, once you get it, you're fine and the lesson really sticks. If you get too much information at once, the brain can't break it all down. Sometimes lessons can go too fast and you need that aide as a back-up. You are seated by the studious children. This is because you mimic their actions. For instance, if you didn't hear quite hear everything the teacher has asked, you look to the other children for cues. If they are turning the page you will mimic that action. Unfortunately you will also mimic bad behavior.

Today the woman in charge of running your I.E.P. told me that you only need a part-time aide. I was very upset over this. I knew I was going to have to assert myself with her, even though we were in front of a 13-member team. I asked her, "If I were to put five pictures of different students on this table would you be able to tell me which one was my son?" She politely answered "no." Then I said, "Don't tell me what my son needs. I'm his mother and I'm also a part of this team here at Elsie Johnson. If you don't find him a full time aide I will be applying for the job." I could tell she didn't know quite how to take me. That morning was really bad for us. Maybe it was to get me ready for that moment. I had tried to get you ready for school and you were having **a huge tantrum.** I was reduced to tears. In frustration, I swatted you on the butt. I had an enormous feeling of losing control and I ran into the front yard and started bawling. Laura, our neighbor, ran over when she saw me outside crying my eyes out. Thank God for my neighbors. She got you ready and insisted that I walk off the frustration. MAN I wish I had someone to relate to. At times I feel so alone. I'm sorry that this happened. I'm looking for anything that can lead me to the answers we need.

Rhonda's Note

As far as giving advice when it comes to the Individualized Education Program (IEP) meeting, you know your own child best. Don't let anyone tell you what's right for your child, especially if you feel it's wrong. Speak up. I did. My best advice to other parents is to come to these meetings informed. The Internet contains a wealth of information about autism and IEPs. Many school systems unfortunately base recommendations on money and budgets. If there is a diagnosis like Jordan's, there are things those individuals are entitled to receive. What my son needed was a full-time teacher's aide. I made sure his needs were met.

Excerpt Teacher Miss Patti

I had the wonderful opportunity to be Jordan's first and second grade teacher. Jordan was part of my looping class. Looping classes keep the same students and teacher together for two years. This was a great program for Jordan because it had the same group of children for two years. He was able to form stronger relationships and develop a higher level of trust with his classmates. They were all more willing to take chances and had a better understanding of each other's strengths and weaknesses.

October 6, 1999 (Jordan's seventh birthday)

We had your 7th birthday party with friends at Chuck E. Cheese in the afternoon and a family one at home in the evening. Auntie Jo, your Godmother, bought you a bowling ball. You were so happy. It seems like your communication is getting better. That's something to be grateful for.

October 14, 1999

Today you started a program at school called Fast Forward. I guess it's supposed to change the neurological processing in the brain to help you receive messages more effectively. They say it will speed up your progress in speech and language by two to four years. Awesome! By the way, that is your latest word "awesome." You've had your first two lessons of Fast Forward and the teachers were floored at how well you do on the computer and how bright you are. Miss Elaine, your aide, is the sweetest woman. She could be your adopted Grandma. She went on to tell me you had her roaring with laughter. You have these head-phones on and you have an allotted time to finish. Not realizing others can hear you, you say loudly "Oh Jesus, I'll get this next man."

December 1, 1999

This is very strange. You have an adult tooth coming in behind the baby tooth. I'm taking you to get it pulled and I'm very worried about your reaction. All your molars have come in at once. This has been an uncomfortable experience for you. Jordan, you are so compassionate, you push my hair back from my forehead and tell me you love me. You still sleep with us. You need and beg for "snuggles." I have to practically wrap myself around you and wait for you to fall asleep. You are also afraid of the dark, and need a light on. If there isn't a light on you cry, "I scary Mom, I scary."

December 5, 1999

Today I yelled at and spanked your dog. You became very upset and told me I was being "destructive" and asked me not to do it again. Dad swore at me and you cried. You can't stand it when we fight.

December 25, 1999

You became sick last night with a mild case of the flu. We went to the Muros today, and Christmas Eve was excellent. You believe in Santa. Then you proceeded to get sick there. On the way home I told you what my Dad used to tell us as kids, "Hey, look in the sky! Did you see Santa?" I thought this was a great tool to get you into bed because that meant Santa was close by. This morning you awoke with excitement even though you didn't get two things that you really wanted.

March 28, 2000

Today you re-memorized the presidents of the United States. This is incredible (and you did it effortlessly).

March 30, 2000

You and your dad went to meet Hulk Hogan and you got his autograph. You were so excited you could hardly contain yourself. You asked if he would sign your hat and he said, "Sure, little dude."

May 21, 2000

You have been testing others in school a lot lately. It seems as though you're beginning to think for yourself too. You will stand by my side and if Daddy tells you I've done something wrong, you'll take my side and say, "No way Dad, my Mom wouldn't do that. She's an angel."

You are continuing to mimic. Unfortunately, there's a little boy whose behavior you shouldn't be mimicking. When you play with this boy you come home acting out his actions. It's so hard for me to deal with that. I need to think about what I can do! I've decided that limiting your playtime is the best answer, seeing as how I've been monitoring your playtime anyway. Every Monday after school I take you bowling. You are very into it. There is a problem; however, if you don't score over 100. You begin to have a meltdown. It's rather embarrassing. Everyone turns to watch you have this temper tantrum that I can't control.

May 29, 2000
Dad and I are helping you learn your states and capitals. I asked you what the capital of Hawaii was and you said "Halahoohoo."

July 11, 2000
Hey, Jordan, you bowled a 179 today!!! Without bumpers! You started screaming in the bowling alley: "I'm so good, I'm so good!" Kids at the bowling alley were flipping. You also are shooting baskets; eight out of 10 throws make it into the hoop. A lot of boys seem intimidated by your ability and don't want to play basketball with you. Your cousin Krystal taught you how to do a back flip on the trampoline Uncle Ed got you. Now you continuously back flip.

August 1, 2000
I asked what you might like for your birthday and you answered, "I think I want Britney Spears, Mommy." You crack me up.

September 6, 2000
Today you told me you think "out of your mind." You told me of a man you said you knew in 1915. You told me how old he was then and you said he was still alive today because he ate healthy. When I got home I asked Daddy if you were right with the math. He said you were and wanted to know

why. I told him the story and he started quizzing you with ages. You were right every time. Freaky! Also your Daddy and I were talking before we went to sleep. You were sound asleep and then you began to talk crystal clear in what we could only guess was Hebrew. We were freaking out again! We kept saying, "Did you hear that?!" It sounded like you definitely knew what you were saying.

September 15, 2000

You are reading a lot of wrestling books. When I was working out today, you came downstairs and started working out along with me. Your hair is past your shoulders so you look like a wrestler. Today, you want to be a professional wrestler and you asked if I would accompany you into the ring. You've got a life size picture of Goldberg on your door. All my clients have to be measured up against him. (He's 6'4"). You make them stand next to the poster, then you record their height and send them on their way. You're so silly.

October 1, 2000

Jordan, you lost your front tooth today and you are so happy. Later on today I caught you with a pair of pliers trying to pry the other tooth out!

October 24, 2000

We took you to a Haunted House. It scared you so much you cried. When you walked out you said, "Mom that scared the crap out of me." Jordan you are something else. For Halloween you are The Undertaker, one of your favorite wrestlers. You went out with Dad to Mike's house and came home with over 300 pieces of candy. I helped out at school and had fun at your party. You love having me around at school.

<u>December 27, 2000</u>

Today we went to Wal-Mart and bought a girl (your first real crush) a gift for Christmas. We then went to the Wheaton Bowl where you played your favorite arcade game and got a 300! There were about 10 of your games up on the arcade with scores higher than 250. The employee there said adults couldn't even make that score. We had a great Christmas. We were watching Who Wants to Be a Millionaire today. You were selecting the order before the question was being asked. Daddy and I were amazed at how you got so many right. We asked you how you did it and you said, "I thinked it with my brain." You still believe in Santa so I manipulate you a little, sorry! I tell you that the elves are looking in your windows to make sure you are being good and doing your chores. I wanted you to do something the other day and you were giving me a hard time about it. So I told you a story Grandma had told me. You still won't sleep in your own bed, so we had one of our friends call you and pretend to be Santa. Your face went from a smile to a frown while you were on the phone with him. I asked what was wrong and you said with big puppy dog eyes that Santa wanted you to be a big boy and sleep in your own bed. For eight years you have shared our bed, and now you're growing and our quarters are becoming tight. Grandma Linda had Christmas day, and you made out like a bandit! I hear you singing as I write this…. "I can see clearly now the rain is gone."

<u>March 16, 2001</u>

Your fifth tooth is loose. It's the one next to the bottom two front ones. You are doing really well in school. Today you finished reading a book on Abraham Lincoln and you, proudly, in class answered the questions about his birth. I just turned 40 and you told me that I was 40 and beautiful! One of my goals with you is to try to teach you compassion for others. It is so important that you grow up to be a kind young man. This seems to be working. Your favorite cereal is Cocoa Krispies, and you are overly excited that you will be receiving a hot lunch at school with chocolate milk. You still want to become a wrestler and the name you picked out is She Go. Dad said he'll call you She Go 801. That happens to be the Pay-per-view channel Daddy and his friends watch. I sing Tina Turner's song, 'You're simply the best...you're different than all the rest, better than anyone, anyone I ever met.' And I mean it.

April 5, 2001

I am having a very hard time getting you to study. I tried offering you money for incentives and you are not biting. You shared information today. It doesn't happen that often so I love it when you do share. You came in second in a spelling bee.

April 14, 2001

Jordan, you bowled for first place on your league this morning. All night you kept talking to yourself. You do that a lot. You tell yourself "I need to stay focused." You came in second place and you cried and cried. You were upset with Dad because he convinced you that oatmeal was the breakfast of champions and you ate oatmeal and didn't come in first. You cried most of the day. And you vowed never to eat oatmeal again. Every night, Jordan, I tell you how much I love you. I love you more than words can express. Sometimes I get the feeling we agreed to this life together on earth so we can share this wonderful experience.

You have taught me so much and you continue to teach me. You call me "your love" and "your sweetie." When you were an infant I would rock you and sing "Let me call you sweetheart." You would listen so intently that I would often wonder if we had danced to that song before. Who knows. All I know is that you are awesome. You snuggle with Dad and me. You want us all very close. I love your little breath blowing on me as you sleep.

May 21, 2001

Music; you love music. You are dancing around today shaking and wiggling your butt. You are laughing big belly laughs. You're so cute. You had a rough day today. Some of the children you play with are resenting that they have to play by your rules. Some of the games are kickball and baseball. I went to the gym teacher to see if there were rules and if she would help me teach them to you. The school is backing me up on this and I only hope it works.

Rhonda's Note

As second grade came to an end, I couldn't help remembering our visit to Dr. Swisser five years ago. He predicted that most of Jordan's outward signs of autism would disappear by this age. Jordan no longer felt the need to pass things past his eyes, watch his heels or his shadows as he ran marathons around the block. Many other repetitive behaviors ceased and tantrums became further apart. I was so pleased with Jordan's progress, I wrote Dr. Swisser a letter to share the good news and thank him for his contribution.

June 26, 2001

What a fast moving summer so far. You love baseball and basketball and will play with anyone. It seems like you have a great love of sports. It amazes me how much knowledge you have acquired in such a short period of time. It's scary. You have make believe baseball games and basketball games everyday. It's almost as if this stimulates you. You love the Sox and the Lakers and you cheer very loud for these teams. We got to go to a Cubs game thanks to Aunt Phyllis and they won!! Your teacher, Miss Patti came over today and you kept calling her "Patti." She didn't mind, but I was a bit embarrassed. This is your last year with Miss Patti and your teacher's aide. I'm going to miss them both so much. We've been very lucky Jordan. Each teacher has been hand picked by his or her successor and, as God always does, the next right person is put on our path. Miss Patti has chosen Miss Beth to be your next teacher. I hear she's fabulous and smiles real big!

Jordan and friend Ankur

8

Where's Jordan?
Group Integration Complete

<u>July 29, 2001</u>
We're still having some issues with you playing kick ball. Three of us moms put our heads together and came up with this option. You have three chances to play nice or you have to go home and can't play with the boys that day. You also get a warning before you start to play so you can remember the rules. It's taken a couple of days but I believe you have it. I took you and two of your friends for Pokémon cards- you guys were so excited.

<u>July 30, 2001</u>
Your highest bowling game yet: 176. I am so proud of you. And you aren't even nine yet.

<u>August 2001</u>
We've had another jam packed month. Swimming, White

Sox game (against Daddy's principles), movies, gymnastics, Great America, carnivals and the list goes on and on. The main thing I have found is that you benefited so much from being placed into groups at an early age. It took awhile to integrate you into the group and get you to participate. You've truly benefited by us constantly trying to get you into group activities.

September 2001

You are bowling on two leagues. You play on Friday nights with Dad and on Saturday mornings. You're losing your teacher's aide. You're struggling with the change. Your classmate Katelynn's mom said you asked Katelynn to marry you. Quite the gentleman: you brought her flowers!

Excerpt 3rd Grade Teacher Miss Beth

The year I spent with Jordan was a remarkable one for me. It gave me the opportunity to grow as a professional, as this was my first experience with a child with Autism. I also treasured every minute with this very gifted and capable child. We have a bond now that I'm sure will last for a lifetime.

In the spring of Jordan's second grade year, I attended a Special Services Team meeting that helped me to become familiar with Jordan's educational plan. I was so impressed with Rhonda from the first moment I heard her speak about her son. She was at the time, and remains to this day, an advocate for Jordan's needs. She was firm, calm, and very informed about what was best for her child. The only weakness I sensed from our first meeting was one that I could entirely identify with as a mother myself. I could tell she felt some discomfort because she didn't know me and probably worried about whether I would be willing to work with her and help her child. There was nothing I could do but earn her trust once the new school year commenced.

Jordan's third grade year proved to be one in which he demonstrated a lot of growth. At the beginning of the year, he wrote brief sentences and had difficulty following through with a thought. I used a structured approach with planners and graphic organizers when teaching writing. The system worked. He became quite fluent with his writing and enjoyed following the plan. He ended up meeting the state standards on the Illinois "ISAT" test! I'll never forget how proud he would be upon finishing a paper. He simply amazed me. Jordan processed his prompts, organized his thoughts and would write nonstop until he was done.

Reading comprehension was a weakness for Jordan, but he became hooked on the Accelerated Reader Program we use at our school and made progress. He read fervently every day and enjoyed the challenge of taking the quizzes that accompanied each book. I remember how disappointed he was when our school library closed for the year in June! We made special arrangements for him to continue the AR Program throughout the summer so that he could satisfy his need to read.

Math was Jordan's greatest strength and he amazed the other children with the way he was able to process numbers and algorithms in his head. I was happy that he had this gift because it helped his self-esteem a great deal. Every single day he was able to shine and it gave him a lot of confidence. Jordan also excelled during class meetings in which we discussed the pillars of character we teach in association with the Character Counts! Program. He possesses an admirable sense of justice and was able to articulate examples of right and wrong.

In closing, I just have to comment on what a tremendous parent Rhonda is. She has always worked tirelessly with Jordan, and he has blossomed with her guidance and support. To this day, she is always quick to admit that she doesn't know everything and sometimes struggles in school herself. She has always been willing to try; however, and as a result, Jordan is a young man who is successful in school and has a bright future.

October 2001

It's your birthday week. You are nine years old. You got yet another bowling ball (you are bowling amazingly well) and Pokémon cards from your Grandma Linda. She took you out with her and you came home very happy. It is so wonderful to see how much your life has turned around. You had fourteen friends at the bowling alley for your party.

Christmas Holidays 2001

The holidays were extra special this year. Jordan still believes in Santa and he has become more group orientated. Dad and I can relax now.

February 2002

Daddy and I were very fortunate to go with you on your Field Museum field trip. You love history and it was a great trip for reading. You are still snuggling in our bed. How much longer? I asked you this and you said you thought you'd be 20 and I'd be 75.

Rhonda's Note
During 2002-2003 I found it very difficult to find the time to write in our journal. I actually have very few concerns and it's a great feeling to look at what I have written, as I have recorded the many highlights of our lives. Preserving the

childhood memories was my original intent. Like in the story of Pinocchio, Jordan has turned into a real boy. Through God's grace many hands were involved.

I believe teachers have one of the hardest jobs there is. They have the ability to mold our children. I knew it would take teamwork and tenacity to make sure my child would flourish. I also knew that I couldn't expect the school system and the teachers to do it all.

Rick and I took our responsibilities very seriously so we made sure we had the correct follow-through on the home front to ensure Jordan's success. I became a team player. I made myself accessible to the teachers by helping them with what they needed on a weekly basis. In return I got to see what was working for Jordan in the classroom and what wasn't working. This also gave me a rapport with the teachers and the teacher's aides each year. We've still remained friends. Building a good foundation through 1.) Assessments, 2.) Early Intervention, and 3.) Preschool Special Education is crucial.

One teacher in particular started an integration program for special needs children at the regular kindergarten class. Miss Joanne was the first to note how Jordan needed to model others and observed how he was wired for learning. The school "Looping" program, keeping students with the same teacher in first and second grades, was ideal, since change is hard for Jordan and this gave him the stability and chance to feel secure in a structured environment.

This also gave his teacher, Miss Patti a chance to assess Jordan's challenges and see where he was excelling. Jordan really loved his third grade teacher Miss Beth. Miss Beth was hand picked by Miss Patti as a teacher who would be excellent for Jordan. She broke the class up for micro moments and would tell stories about her own little boy and husband. Jordan would come home and repeat these stories to me. My boy's communication began to develop very quickly and I know it was because he loved school and learning from Miss Beth.

Miss Beth followed suit and handpicked Miss Barbara. This was important because Miss Barbara was known for building good character. It was vital that Jordan learned to treat his fellow students with kindness and respect. This gave Jordan an opportunity to shine. Jordan loved that he was challenged to be the best person he could be and dutifully remains true to the lessons Miss Barbara passed on to him. Miss Barbara was also heavily focused on expressive reading and writing. Language is very difficult for Jordan, but he seems to have walked away with not only a grasp of it, but also a love of both language and arts.

In fifth grade Jordan and I met his teacher Miss Lisa (hand picked by Miss Barbara). Miss Lisa was not only right for Jordan, she was also right for me. She was very organized and structured and gave me the confidence that I could now "pull back." This was exceptionally important since junior high school is right around the corner.

Jordan was also blessed to have a speech teacher named Miss Julie. The interesting thing about Miss Julie's teaching is that she made our experience into a triangle adventure. Together a teacher's aide, Miss Julie and I could be consistently backing up the material and learning methods. Miss Julie also helped by modifying his tests. Jordan needs things broken down and can't have too many answers to choose from. Otherwise he becomes overwhelmed.

The person at the helm of the educational pyramid is the principal of the school, Miss Cathy. She has dedicated her life to her school as do most principals. What sets her apart is that she interviewed each teacher's aide, and handpicked the one who would fit into Jordan's learning style. Miss Cathy has over-seen Jordan's education, experienced his confusion, and most of all had the patience to put up with me.

When it comes to Jordan, I was just pushing for the best that I could get him. I felt like I was his only advocate and I couldn't let him down. We were lucky, as you can see, to have all the support of friends, family and educators at the right time and in the right place!

Friends Connor and Ankur with Jordan

9

What You Love and What Loves You

<u>June 2003</u>
I don't understand a lot about baseball. This is your Rookie year and, not knowing what was to come, you ended up on a wonderful team of very nice boys with a wonderful coach. The team you play for is the Cardinals. The coaching staff agrees you should be one of four who will be chosen for the All-Star Team. As a Rookie this doesn't happen often. Daddy said a coach's son will usually be chosen, since they work more often giving personal one-on-one to their own sons. This time you were chosen. You were the lead-off batter of the All-Star Game and you had 23 hits for the season. You also received the game ball for Most Valuable Player for your game performance. This is what I describe as an out of body experience. No one knows who you are much less who I am and as I am walking around I hear everyone talking about you. "Who is that kid?" they ask.

"Did you see his sweet swing?" "What!? A rookie with 23 hits, wow!" I want to tell you, Jordan, I was elated, proud, joyful and so very grateful to be your Mom.

Excerpt Baseball Coach Chuck

The 2003 baseball season approached with the usual chatter among the previous season coaches. As managers, we were now entering the 10-year-old level, which meant that most of us have managed with and against each other in the previous five seasons.

A night or two before the draft, a couple of us met to discuss the available players and share information on the talented kids. We also discuss the "sleeper picks" in the draft, the troublesome parents and what we may know about the unrated kids. The unrated players are either new to the sport or new to the community. At the very least, they did not play in the community the previous season and, therefore, did not have a skill rating assigned to them. One of the not rated players was Jordan. He had a note next to his name...Autism.

There were 11 teams in the draft and 122 available players in the draft. I believe there were eight not rated players. As the draft progresses, the ones that remain are not rated players along with a few low-skills rated players. These remaining players have their names placed into a hat and are distributed via a blind draw. On this day, Jordan was one of the names in that hat.

Coach Keith and I worked our way through the draft assembly and we had a pretty good team. For the most part, we knew all the kids and all the parents. Our experiences showed that the chemistry of the parents is almost more important than the ability of the kids in making the season a positive one. Keith and I admitted to ourselves that we knew nothing about Autism or its different levels. Our extra blind pick was the absolute last player selected last season: Jordan Brunett.

Keith and I shrugged our shoulders and we figured we would do our best with Jordan. This was Jordan's first season and we could tell he was very excited about baseball. He seemed a little more excited than the other boys. We handed out the uniforms and he was grinning from ear to ear. At practice Jordan was comparable to the other kids. At the end of first practice I would hit fly balls until one of the kids made a catch. Jordan made the first catch. Rick, Jordan's dad, was on hand to help us instruct Jordan with multiple instructions. We wanted to make sure Jordan didn't become confused, which would then hamper his performance. With that advice, Keith, who worked the batting drills with the kids, would pace the instructions to Jordan one at a time. Jordan had a natural swing and we didn't want to alter that. We had come to find out that Rick has pitched probably a thousand balls to Jordan getting him prepared for organized baseball. In addition, Jordan enjoyed watching baseball on television, which explained his 'TV' swagger.

In his first game, Jordan batted in the bottom third of the line-up and went about three for four, displaying some power, but a good quick bat. This success was not a one-time wonder. Jordan started at the lead-off position for the next game and stayed there for the rest of the season! He ended the season with a near 500 batting average and very few strikeouts. Jordan also organized a group of 12-year-olds to come over to the field behind his house to play baseball. What began as a blind pick ended up being one of the 'feel goods' of the season. Even the other managers in the league wanted to meet this kid who had never played the game.

If there is a downside to this, it is the fact that it will be difficult for me to get Jordan Brunett on my 11-year old team. Jordan is no longer a secret. In the past season the only information given was autism. The information now given to coaches will still start with the letter A...but this time for All-Star."

Excerpt 4th Grade Teacher Miss Barbara

Jordan: peaceful, joyful, kind and caring, living in the now, without conflict, enjoying friends, living integrity, and always wanting what is best. These are some of the attributes of this delightful child. But there was another quality that superceded the others. It was his sunshine. It was like the radiance that comes from a sunbeam. How do you describe this particular sunbeam?

There are sunbeams and there are those that bring in clouds. Sometimes children come into a classroom with preconceived ideas of what fourth grade will be. Sometimes they bring marvelous self-esteem. However, there are others that bring the lack of self-esteem from their previous record in the school system or preconceived ideas about their ability or lack of abilities. Jordan, however, had the radiance of a sunbeam. That was my initial impression of Jordan. From the first day to the last, I discovered a child who radiated what all teachers want in their students—a willingness to shine in their own way and to be what they were meant to be: intelligent, creative and responsible. He came into my class with openness to new ideas, a willingness to try them and the joy that goes with discovering new things. This trusting soul came with his own self-empowerment.

I loved watching Jordan, especially in the library. His goal was to raise his reading level. Since sunbeams do not know about darkness, Jordan likewise went about voraciously gathering and reading books with the light of enthusiasm and remarkable personal motivation. During our Sustained Silent Reading time he memorized messages from the books. You could tell it was a love affair with reading because he always shared his reading score with me. It was always 80 percent or higher. I loved those moments where he felt the radiant energy of the remarkable ability to spontaneously calculate numbers.

Jordan had the marvelous ability to do very difficult mathematical calculations without using paper and pencil. I loved calling on Jordan to quickly help our class by almost instantaneously calculating difficult computations during social studies or other subjects. This kept the flow of the instruction unimpeded by paper and pencil computation. I knew the joy he felt in being able to share his natural ability to quickly compute numbers.

Another quality that I truly valued in Jordan was his integrity. Teachers are always working on character education. Educators know that ability is magnified when one has a standard of criteria of decency and honesty to draw from. Jordan was also fully equipped in this area. One incident I specifically remember was at recess time when our class and another class were playing kickball. In this incident a child in our class was accused of swearing and acting belligerently in a way that is not in accordance with the principles of our school. This child was wrongfully accused and Jordan knew it. When he came home from school he told his mom about the episode. She in turn related the information to me. When I asked Jordan about it he said he would willingly stand up for this child and go to the principal so that justice would be done. He wasn't afraid of taking a stand for the truth for he knew an injustice was done and must be rectified. The wrongfully accused child felt the burden lifted off of his shoulders and this act of integrity returned his faith in our school system's method of honestly dealing fairly with children's problems. This ray of light shining with trustworthiness and truthfulness benefited our classroom. This whole school has benefited from Jordan's stand for justice.

Excerpt Speech Pathologist Miss Julie

As a Speech Language Pathologist, I have had the pleasure of working with Jordan over the past four school years. My first memory of Jordan was at the beginning of his second grade year. I was his new speech therapist that year, and it was one of my first sessions with him. Jordan told me he wanted to show me a "trick" that he could do. He was able to calculate the year someone was born when given their current age, or if given the age, he was able to tell me the year they were born. He was able to do this in a matter of seconds. I was amazed at how quickly, he as a second grader, was able to do this. It was an area of strength for Jordan at that time, and he wanted to show me that. As I worked with Jordan, I came to realize that things that were concrete in method or form (such as Math computations) were much easier for Jordan to comprehend than the abstract. I remember thinking on that first day that Jordan's speech skills were very good and that he communicated pretty well with the routine social interaction. It was when I probed deeper and beyond the routine social questions that Jordan demonstrated more difficulty. Jordan has made much improvement over the years. For instance, he used to have much difficulty answering and discriminating between "who, what, where, when, and why" questions whereas now he has little to no difficulty in this area. He would also make comments in conversation that to him made sense, but left the listener lost because he left off important details (such as "who" he was talking about, referring to "she", but the listener didn't know who "she" was). He has made great improvements in these areas of social communication and expressive language skills.

He has learned social rules and when to appropriately apply them over time. Jordan does tend to take language very literally and still has some difficulty with figurative language or more abstract concepts. He has been taught, for example, what different idioms mean and how to interpret them. He continues to do best in routine or structured situations but is better able to handle changes in schedule or format. With preparation or individual instruction prior to the change in format, Jordan is then able to show his true potential. The use of visual supports when teaching Jordan has also been very helpful. His improvements in the area of reading have been incredible to watch as well. Jordan has surpassed a lot of expectations over the years. His motivation to overcome areas that are more difficult has and continues to be a great strength of his. It has been amazing to watch him learn and grow throughout the years.

Excerpt 5th Grade Teacher Miss Lisa and Teacher's Aide Miss Jan

We have only been working with Jordan for a semester, but in that time we have both learned a lot about him. Math is Jordan's greatest strength! He amazes everyone in the class with his multiplication facts and how quickly he can compute a problem in his head. For the most part, when Jordan doesn't understand something, he catches on quickly. Although reading comprehension is a struggle, it definitely does not keep him from reading. We have a program called Accelerated Reader that keeps Jordan motivated to read. He reads every chance he gets in order to reach his goal. He reads about a book every night.

Writing is the area where Jordan has the most difficulty. It is very hard for him to put his thoughts down on paper. The best thing that we have learned to do is help him process his answer before even picking up a pen. Jordan has become more responsible and independent in filling out his assignment note-book and he always has his homework in on time.

Jordan is a joy to have this year! He tries so hard and never gives up, even when he is frustrated with a concept. We have both learned a lot from his year. Jordan wouldn't be who he is today if he didn't have the parents that he does. They spend hours work-ing with him and that is why Jordan is so successful in school!

2004 From Dad to Jordan

I knew long before you were born that you'd be special. It took mom and me so long to conceive you that when you finally arrived I thought I'd be ready for anything. Little did I know. While my buddies told me that I'd be counting fingers and toes in the hospital, as we went along our way I knew that the impor-tant thing I wanted to teach you was how to love. But a funny thing happened along the way… you taught me how to love like I never believed a human could.

I was hoping you would be a sports enthusiast, since sports built character in my youth and kept me out of trouble. At an early age you took a liking to wrestling. Your first ballgame was at Wrigley Field at ten months old. I remember your first Sox game at one and a half. We stayed for the fireworks display after the game and the noise and loud sounds made you literally crawl into a corner and take cover. I covered you as best I could until it ended. I felt terrible for you because you were so distraught with the loud noises.

Your interest in wrestling grew as you did. You couldn't speak, but together we traveled the suburbs and inner city to hunt for die-cast wrestling cars issued in 1997-1998. We finally completed this in late '98. I never needed to keep a list; you knew exactly what cars you had. You were older and wiser than your age. I would never have believed a 5 or 6-year-old could comprehend collectibles. I explained to you these were for looking at and we couldn't open them up. I did purchase some duplicates for you to play with though. You would spend hours and days playing with the cars in the boxes. Arranging and rearranging them.

I'd move them if you stepped away from them and upon your return you would have a fit and put them back into their original order.

I will always remember when the show Married with Children would come on. You were one year old then and in your bouncy chair. As soon as you'd hear the theme song start you'd start whimpering until your chair was put in front of the television. We at first thought there was something wrong with your hearing but we noticed that you were moving your head to the beat.

Jordan, one of my concerns was how other children would view you because you were different. As I grew up, kids could really be tough on other kids.

Your Mom and I tried to instill in you self-esteem and self-confidence. I believe sports helped a lot with this. We are always telling you how smart and handsome you are and how special you are. We never stop telling you how lucky we are to have you. I've tried to teach you that there are no shortcuts in life. Especially, in sports. Play fair and never cheat to win. You have to learn to be a good loser to become a champion or a great winner. You're very competitive and I've tried to teach you to compete in everything in life. Competition is challenge…winning is a celebration, but handling defeat is just as important. You've learned at an early age what commitment is.

I will not be the parent that makes you play all sports, instruments, or makes you go to church and the like. However, if you commit to anything, I've taught you to complete it from start to finish. Like it or not. I will not live my childhood through you but I would love to be part of your growing up.

You seem to tell me everything, and I've taught you to tell the truth and be honest. Communication will be a big part of your future whether you will be able to say exactly what's in that little brain of yours or not. You try and I give you that.

Don't quit, Jordan, please don't ever quit. I love you with every fiber of my being, more than life itself. I was supposed to be the teacher and instead you made me your pupil. Showing me on a daily basis another miracle. With God's grace and more people in your life for a reason, you will succeed to places people have only dreamed of.

Enjoy your journey.
Love, Dad.

2004 From Mom to Jordan

There is no end to you. You made your 500 series in bowling. I'm going to leave this open-ended because I will continue to journal for you. I will end this insert for you. However, by telling you what I tell you every night before bed. We say our prayer. Then I say I love you and you say you love me too. And then I tell you just how proud I am of you and how damn handsome you are! You then tell me that you are proud of me and I'm so pretty. Then I tell you that I'm so glad you chose me to be your Mom.

One time you said that you almost picked a Japanese Mom and Dad but you didn't think you wanted to speak just Japanese. So you chose us instead. Then you say "Mom, I'm so glad I picked you because I'm so very happy." What more could I ask for? Xoxoxoxox Mommy,

I love you sooooo much, Jordan.

Conclusion

October 2004—Jordan turns 12 years old and is integrated into a normal classroom setting. He excels in baseball and bowling. In 2003 Jordan played in the Little League All-Star game and received the game ball for the most hits in the league. Most recently in bowling, Jordan had a 587 series that advanced him to a Tournament in downstate Illinois in which he placed seventh in the state! Jordan has proven to be an awesome boy and a true…All-Star!

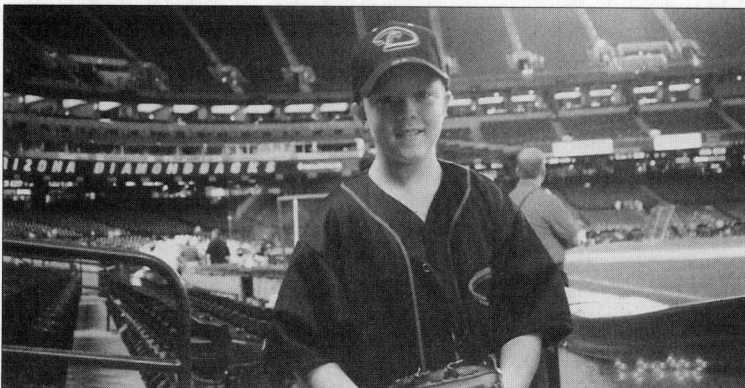

References

Highly Recommended Books

The OASIS guide to Asperger Syndrome by Patrica Romanowski
Bashe and Barbara L. Kirby
*Targeting Autism: What We Know, Don't Know, and Can Do To
Help Young Children with Autism and Related Disorders.*
By Shirley Cohn
Emergence: Labeled Autistic By Temple Grandin
Asperger's Syndrome: A Guide For Parents and Professionals
By Tony Attwood
Asperger Syndrome and Difficult Moments Practical Solutions for
Tantrums, Rage, and Meltdowns by Brenda Smith Myles and
Jack Southwick

Highly Recommended Web Sites

www.cureautismnow.com How You Can Help Find A Cure.
www.maapservices.org/index.html MAAP Services for Autism
and Asperger Spectrum
www.autismsociety.org Local Chapter Listings/Autism Society
of America
www.naar.org National Alliance for Autism Research
www.aspergersyndrome.org OASIS- Online Asperse
Syndrome Support and Information
www.autism2allstar.com Power Point Presentation for
Teachers and Parents of Asperger's/PDD and the support group Support
Parents and Empower Asperger's/Autistic Kids (SPEAK).

Practitioner Referral

www.autism.com/ari/dan/contents.html is the DAN (Defeat Autism Now)
web site that doctors who are familiar with autism and treatments attend con-
ferences on further learning and research for autistic children. This site contains a list of practitioners all over the world. DAN is an ongoing project of the
Autism Research Institute.

Rhonda Brunett and husband Rick kept a journal of their only child Jordan since first finding out they were expecting. Little did they know, that what began as a loving way to preserve family memories, would result in a documentary of Jordan's life as an Autistic child.

From 1992 to 2004 including pregnancy, early childhood detection and up to the functional happy boy Jordan is today, Rhonda kept a journal of the details. She documented the trials and tribulations that one could only imagine on a day-to-day, week-to-week and at times, month-to-month basis.

It was suggested that the journal and videotape library serve as a wonderful tool for experiencing the challenges that often surround the lives of a family with an Autistic child.

Due to much encouragement, combined with the apparent lack of layman's materials on Autism, Rhonda was fueled to write From Autism to All-Star.

The personal observations and commentary of friends, family, teachers and the medical profession from Jordan's exterior and social environment are also included.

Rhonda's objective: to share their experiences and challenges, thereby helping to give readers some insight…and discover something that will give them or someone they know, answers to questions, solace and hope.

To contact Rhonda Brunett
Autism2allstar@yahoo.com